A MAN SMILES
AT DEATH
WITH
HALF A FACE

José Rodrigues Miguéis in 1942, just before his stay in Beth Israel Hospital.
Courtesy of John Hay Library, Brown University.

A MAN SMILES
AT DEATH
WITH
HALF A FACE

José Rodrigues Miguéis

Translated and with an Introduction by
George Monteiro

Brown University Press

Published by University Press of New England
Hanover and London

The University Press of New England
is a consortium of universities in New England dedicated to publishing
scholarly and trade works by authors from member campuses and elsewhere. The New England imprint signifies uniform standards for
publication excellence maintained without exception by the consortium
members. A joint imprint of University Press of New England and a
sponsoring member acknowledges the publishing mission of that university and its support for the dissemination of scholarship throughout the
world. Cited by the American Council of Learned Societies as a model to
be followed, University Press of New England publishes books under its
own imprint and the imprints of

Brandeis University

Brown University

Clark University

University of Connecticut

Dartmouth College

University of New Hampshire

University of Rhode Island

Tufts University

University of Vermont

Wesleyan University

Printed in the United States of America

Library of Congress Cataloging-in-Publication Data on page 81.

IN MEMORIAM

Doctor Francisco Pulido Valente,
master teacher of physicians and men,

and

Doctor Luís Navarro Soeiro,
a great heart in the service of souls

J. R. M.

This translation is dedicated to
Onésimo Teotónio Almeida

G. M.

Contents

Note on the Text

The publication history of *Um Homem Sorri à Morte—Com Meia Cara (A Man Smiles at Death with Half a Face)* begins with its serialization, in thirteen installments, in the magazine supplement of the newspaper *Diário de Lisboa*. The first installment appeared on July 19, 1958. The next eleven installments appeared in successive weeks. The thirteenth installment appeared on October 17, 1958, two weeks after the twelfth installment. Paged consecutively (1–52), it was subtitled "Novela." On his own copy of the magazine pages, now part of the José Rodrigues Miguéis Collection at Brown University, the author has crossed out "Novela" and written in "Narrativa." In book form the narrative was brought out by the Lisbon publisher Estúdios Cor, in February 1959. The same publisher brought out a second edition, lightly revised, in July 1965. A third edition, following the text of the second edition, was published by Editorial Estampa, Lisbon, in December 1984. *A Man Smiles at Death with Half a Face* follows the text of the third edition.

Among holograph materials in the José Rodrigues Miguéis Collection at Brown University are four consecutive pages (from the middle of the second chapter) of the author's manuscript for this work.

Bibliographical Note

There has been some important work done on José Rodrigues Miguéis in English. A model of its kind is John Austin Kerr, Jr.'s bio-bibliography, *Miguéis—To the Seventh Decade,* Romance Monographs No. 29 (University, Mississippi: Romance Monographs, 1977). A collection of critical essays that includes the proceedings of an international symposium on Miguéis held at Brown University in 1981 as well as some other material either pertaining to the author or by him was published as *José Rodrigues Miguéis: Lisbon in Manhattan,* ed. Onésimo T. Almeida (Providence, R. I.: Gávea-Brown, 1984). A selection of Miguéis' short fiction in English translation by various hands was published as *Steerage and Ten Other Stories,* ed. George Monteiro (Providence, R. I.: Gávea-Brown, 1983). Jorge de Sena is the author of the biographical article in the *Columbia Dictionary of Modern European Literature,* 2nd edition, ed. J. A. Bédé and William B. Edgerton (New York: Columbia University Press, 1980), pp. 535–36. There are two unpublished dissertations done in the United States: John A. Kerr, Jr.'s "Aspects of Time, Place and Thematic Content in the Prose Fiction of José Rodrigues Miguéis as Indications of the Artist's Weltansicht" (University of Wisconsin, 1970), and Maria Angelina Duarte's "Social Political Undercurrents in Four Works by José Rodrigues Miguéis" (University of Minnesota, 1980).

Reviews of *Um Homem Sorri à Morte—Com Meia Cara* in Portuguese include: (1) Mário Sottomayor Cardia, *O Médico* (Porto) (1959), 313; (2) *Diário de Lisboa* (Apr. 23, 1959); (3) Augusto Abelaira, *Diário Popular* (Lisbon) (Apr. 23, 1959), pp. 6–7, 11; (4)

A República (May 3, 1959); (5) "S.", *Gazeta Musical e de Todas as Artes*, 2nd series, 9 (June 1959), 317; (6) *Jornal de Notícias* (Porto) (June 15, 1959), p. 4; (7) João Maia, *Brotéria* (Lisbon), 69 (July–Dec. 1959), 63–65; (8) Taborda de Vasconcelos, *Diário de Notícias* (Jan. 2, 1966), pp. 17–18; and (9) Oscar Mendes, "Três Livros de Miguéis," *Suplemento Literário, Minas Gerais* (Brazil) (Nov. 20, 1971), p. 10.

Acknowledgments

I wish to thank Camila C. Miguéis, who, as executor of José Rodrigues Miguéis' estate, has kindly given me permission to translate and publish *Um Homem Sorri à Morte—Com Meia Cara*. Her unfailing cooperation and counsel over the years on this and other matters relating to Miguéis has enhanced my pleasure in working on this fine writer.

Thanks, too, are due to my colleagues at the Center for Portuguese and Brazilian Studies, Brown University—Onésimo T. Almeida, Nelson Vieira, and Luiz F. Valente—to Maria Angelina Duarte of the University of Iowa, to Richard Ratzan of the University of Connecticut Medical School and Jeff Grathwohl of the University Press of New England, who early on saw the merit of Miguéis' book and independently encouraged me to translate it into English, to the Calouste Gulbenkian Foundation of Lisbon, which has both directly and indirectly supported my work on Miguéis and other Portuguese writers, to the editors of Gávea-Brown Publications and the *Journal of Medical Humanities,* who have consented to my use of materials first published by them, to Mark Brown and Barbara Filipac of the John Hay Library, who have always facilitated my work with the Miguéis holdings, to Francisco Fagundes of the University of Massachusetts at Amherst, who so promptly and graciously agreed to look over my translation and who did so with dispatch, to Stephen Monteiro, whose attentive reading of the manuscript and subsequent suggestions were most helpful, and to Candida Hutter and Armanda Silva, who have a good deal to do with making the Center for Portuguese and Brazilian Studies so hospitable to faculty and students alike.

G. M.

Providence, Rhode Island, April 1990

Isolato in Manhattan:
An Introduction

I

Among José Rodrigues Miguéis' papers there exists a statement explicitly to the effect that critics have failed to perceive the most important thing about his writing: that it is all autobiographical. Publication of such an admission (or claim) by this Portuguese writer, self-exiled in the United States, would not have stood him in good stead in Portugal during his lifetime nor, one suspects, would it serve to enhance his reputation in Portugal even today, where no one would bother to see what might be behind Miguéis' statement. Surely, he could have meant by the statement (and probably did) that he wrote only about what actually occurred to him. The key though is in discerning what he might have meant by "what happened." The answer to this question, if there is one, is in the fiction itself. What I have in mind, specifically, are those individuals in Miguéis' work, usually the narrators themselves, who spend countless hours in their rooms, in their beds at night, listening to the sounds of the pension, the apartment, the hotel, perceiving by limited cues—old, new—the drama that folds and unfolds. Perception for Miguéis' people in this case works hand-in-glove with the imagination to piece out the narrative of "happenings" outside of the "walls" of his bed. So we see in Miguéis' work, early and late, the figure of the recumbent, restless narrator, mixing memory and desire with the fears of the tender imagination. In this, Miguéis is a bit like the speaker of T. S. Eliot's early poems, something of a Prufrock or the unnamed personae who speak the various parts of "Preludes." Better still, he is like Eliot's younger kindred spirit, Delmore Schwartz.

If not born a New Yorker like his younger American contemporary, Miguéis became one; and his fictional and nonfictional narratives, wherever they are set in time or place, are, like Schwartz's most typical stories and poems, imagined by a dweller in a Manhattan apartment. Think here of the opening passage of what is perhaps Schwartz's most famous (and Eliotian) poem:

> In the naked bed, in Plato's cave,
> Reflected headlights slowly slid the wall,
> Carpenters hammered under the shaded window,
> Wind troubled the window curtains all night long,
> A fleet of trucks strained uphill, grinding,
> Their freights covered, as usual.
> The ceiling lightened again, the slanting diagram
> Slid slowly forth.
> 　　　　　　　　Hearing the milkman's chop,
> His striving up the stair, the bottle's chink,
> I rose from bed, lit a cigarette,
> And walked to the window. The stony street
> Displayed the stillness in which buildings stand,
> The street-lamp's vigil and the horse's patience.
> The winter sky's pure capital
> Turned me back to bed with exhausted eyes.*

Imagination we take for granted in a writer, but memory we give short shrift to. Miguéis' fiction tells us many things, but that memory suffuses all he shows us over and over again. And it is not just the past and primarily the past that feeds memory; it is rather the present that carries us into the past.

José Rodrigues Miguéis' work has been compared to that of the French realists and the late nineteenth-century Russian naturalists. And there is much merit in such comparisons. But I should like to

---

*"In the Naked Bed, in Plato's Cave," in *Summer Knowledge: New and Selected Poems: 1938–1958* (Garden City, N. Y.: Doubleday, 1959), p. 25.

sketch out another possible comparison, one that has nothing to do, I suspect, with either the literary sources of Miguéis' work or any notion that his work shows the influence of his reading. John Steinbeck was, give or take a few years, a contemporary of Miguéis'. Even as Steinbeck, in the 1930s particularly, allied himself with the human crowd of marginalized and social and political immigrants, in such works as *Tortilla Flat, In Dubious Battle, The Grapes of Wrath,* and *Cannery Row,* so, too, did Miguéis, in *O Pão Não Cai do Céu* (a circa 1937 play rewritten as fiction during the 1940s and '50s but not published until after the author's death) and numerous short stories. But unlike Steinbeck, who in *Tortilla Flat* suffused his band of social misfits with touches of Arthurian magic-sparkle, Miguéis saw his "third-class" humanity, when he found it to be such, raw and half-cooked; that is to say that he was more tough-minded about, less programmatically proletarian in his judgments of the humanity under his focused eye. In short, Miguéis did a better job of keeping his politics of humanity out of his fiction in the 1930s and his politics of state out of his fiction in the 1960s, largely saving his political–social pronouncements for his journalism and in-proper-person commentary. In fact, among American writers it was not Steinbeck but Erskine Caldwell who earned Miguéis' greatest respect. "Implacable in his human panoramas, stripped of all false, prefabricated mystery, dry as wood-cuts, and shot through with biting humor," Caldwell, Miguéis asserted in an interview in 1959, "managed to remain faithful to what was human, to be objective, while avoiding the dejection and pessimism of his older fellow-writers. . . . The writer disappears behind his work. But when we do spot him, we see that he is engaged, interested, and fundamentally alone, yet confident in the capacity of men to fend for themselves."*

*Mario Henriques, "José Rodrigues Miguéis, Primeiro Prémio 'Camilo', Afirma: 'Só Pretendo Contar Histórias Simples e Claras!' " *Diário Popular, Quinta-Feira à Tarde* (literary supplement) (July 2, 1959), p. 11.

To a greater extent than John Steinbeck or Erskine Caldwell, José Rodrigues Miguéis was a man of letters in the large European manner, but, like Steinbeck and Caldwell, he will be best remembered, as he would have expected and desired, for his fiction. And as a writer of novels and stories, he will be remembered for his closely observed, accurately detailed memorializations of twentieth-century life in Europe and the United States. An intellectual by temperament and a democrat in spirit and politics, Miguéis rewarded his readers over a long career spanning six decades and ending only with his death in 1980 with a series of richly felt narratives whose core of sentiment was uniquely enhanced by the writer's talent for quick caricature and his propensity for trenchant social criticism. And this is as it should be, for Miguéis was above all a storyteller. It was narrative (even in the autobiographical account *A Man Smiles at Death with Half a Face*) that counted first and foremost, not narrative experimentation, in an age so betaken and bemused and beleaguered by modernist devices and ploys, but stories in themselves told in direct and clear style. Miguéis made no bones about this. "As for style, I am totally indifferent to it," he explained the year before his death; "I tell a story because I like to tell it. For me the style is the subject itself. It is the subject which sets the style, as the substance of a given mineral predetermines the shape into which it must crystallize."* Nowhere in the corpus of Miguéis' fiction are there any examples of what in the same commentary he called, with scarcely withheld derision, "the continued obscurity and structural complexity of certain authors who thirst for novelty and have little to say." The complexity of Miguéis' narratives lies elsewhere: in the psychological realism of his narrators, named and unnamed, and of their observations about the human beings who fall within their ken. Miguéis had at his com-

---

*"Last Word: Miguéis on Miguéis," in *Steerage and Ten Other Stories*, ed. George Monteiro (Providence, R. I.: Gávea-Brown, 1983), p. 222.

mand full knowledge of the grand traditions of Western literature as well as the metastatic experiments of the Modernists (including those of their forebears and heirs) and chose to follow the example of the masters of narrative. Mixing memory with desire in the alembic of his imagination, he saw himself in a line stretching back to Balzac.

II

The author of *A Man Smiles at Death with Half a Face* was born José Claudino Rodrigues Miguéis in Lisbon on December 9, 1901. His father was a native of Galicia, Spain, and his mother of the District of Coimbra. Miguéis was the youngest of three children. His brother, whose death in 1918 in Miguéis' arms is reported in *A Man Smiles at Death*, was born in 1895, while his sister was born in 1898.

Miguéis attended private primary schools in Lisbon (see his first novel, *Páscoa Feliz*, 1932) and graduated from the Liceu Camões. At the University of Lisbon he studied law and was graduated *cum laude*. From his earliest days Miguéis was interested in politics. He never deviated from the staunch republicanism he inherited from his father. His politics would eventually lead to his self-imposed exile in the United States, which began in 1935 and lasted, in effect, until his death in New York City in 1980. During the forty-seven year dictatorship in Portugal, which ended with the revolution of 1974, Miguéis was a strong opponent of first Antonio Oliveira Salazar and later Marcelo Caetano, the latter of whom had been Miguéis' fellow student at the law school.

Between his politics and his interest in writing Miguéis early on discovered that he had little interest in the practice of law. He did not like waiting around for his clients' cases to come up for the judiciary and was easily tempted into writing on behalf of his political causes. Miguéis had several talents—among them were drawing, singing, and acting—but it was writing that was always primary. As he told Camila Campanella, whom he married in 1940 after he had divorced his first wife, "The day I can't write there will be the devil to pay!"

After graduating from the university Miguéis set up an office with two other attorneys. But he did not practice long. He was more interested in writing for the socially conscious journal *Seara Nova* and the newspaper *A República*. By 1929 he had given up his law office and gone to Belgium on a government fellowship to study modern methods of teaching abnormal children. It was there that he met his first wife, Pecia (Pola) Cogan Portnoy. They were married in 1932. In Belgium he stayed in pensions, and the first one he stayed in gave him the background for his story "Leah," written in 1940 and included in *Léah e Outras Histórias* (1958). That stay of three years in Belgium also provided him with material and background for other books such as *Nikalai! Nikalai!* (1971) and *Uma Aventura Inquietante* (1934–36, 1958).

In 1935 he emigrated to the United States, arriving in New York on the 8th of July. Awaiting him in New York City was Camila Pitta Campanella, whom he had met years earlier in Lisbon and with whom he would live for the next forty-five years, until his death in 1980.

In his first years in the United States Miguéis actively pursued his form of politics. He was a founder of the Portuguese Workers Club in Greenwich Village and, according to Camila Miguéis, he contributed political and social commentary to *La Voz*, the Spanish-language daily started by Zeferino Barbazán in 1937 (it lasted until 1939). In 1942 he became a naturalized American citizen. From 1942 until 1951 he worked for the *Reader's Digest*, editing and translating its Portuguese-language edition. In 1942 and again in 1945 he was hospitalized, the first time with peritonitis and the second time with a grievous brain infection, the two illnesses treated in *Um Homem Sorri à Morte—Com Meia Cara* (1958, 1959). In 1946 his collection of stories *Onde a Noite se Acaba* appeared. Another highly autobiographical novel of his Lisbon years, *A Escola do Paraíso,* was published in 1960. More of the stories he was publishing all along in journals and newspapers were collected under the titles of *Gente da Terceira Classe* (1962) and *Comércio Com o Inimigo* (1973). In 1975 he published his two-volume novel, a historical and spiritual allegory, *O Milagre Segundo Salomé.* Appearing just at the time of the successful revolution of April 25, 1974, which overthrew the Salazar–Caetano dictatorship, this novel, perhaps Miguéis' masterpiece, has not yet received the attention it so richly merits. Since his death have appeared, in 1981, *O Pão Não Cai do Céu* (a novel first written as a drama in 1937 or thereabouts), *Paços Confusos,* a collection of stories (1982), and *Idealista no Mundo Real,* a novel (1986).

All the while—down through the decades—he was writing and publishing plays, journalistic chronicles, essays, and translations. Among his translations are Carson McCullers' *The Heart Is a Lonely Hunter,* Erskine Caldwell's *A Lamp for Nightfall,* and F. Scott Fitzgerald's *The Great Gatsby.*

III

In 1935 José Rodrigues Miguéis left Portugal for the United States. He settled in New York City, where he would remain, except for short absences (including a year in Brazil), until his death in 1980 at the age of seventy-nine. In self-imposed exile, he insisted that filling "reams of paper with the unpublishable prose of a Portuguese writer *in partibus infidelium*" was his "way of continuing to live" his "life in Portugal, without actually being there."

Miguéis' fame as a writer rests on his fiction, particularly those stories and novels that draw upon his sometimes tortured memories of his early life in Lisbon and elsewhere. But Miguéis also wrote some nonfictional narrative prose.

The most remarkable example of those "autobiographical narratives" is, perhaps, *A Man Smiles at Death with Half a Face*. Published as a book in 1959, and running a little over a hundred pages of actual text (including the author's preface), this work presents a detailed account of the author's encounter with near-death in 1945.

The narrative is aimed, explains Miguéis, at three audiences:

> [I]t was first of all, for hypochondriacs—those people frightened of sickness and obsessed with termination—that I wrote these pages in my journal; later, for those who want to know the reactions of someone lying in a hospital bed, surrounded by death; and then, perhaps, for those physicians interested in knowing how their patients view them.

He intended it, therefore, to bring news and information to those curious about what it is like to be dangerously ill in hospital and to survive that illness. The book will bring news to those who have not had the experience, whether they be, potentially, patients or administering doctors. The news will be sociological and psychological.

There is much detail about hospital procedures and work patterns, from the infrastructure of the doctors' bedside and clinical rounds to the strategic placement of patients on the neurological ward—the changing and sometimes unchanging positions of their beds indicate whether they are candidates for imminent surgery, for convalescence, or for death. Persistently the screens go up round each of the doomed patients, to be taken down only when the body is ready for removal to the morgue. Obviously such screens are useful in the ward of all hospitals for many procedures other than those of body preparation and removal, but not in this book where their appearance is always ominous.

But the emphasis in *A Man Smiles at Death* is, first and last, on the man of the title, the author, who is the narrator. He never tells us his name or the names of his wife and daughter (though once he is addressed as "Joe"). He does tell us the names of friends, doctors and nurses, and the first names of patients. He tells us that he is a writer and, by trade, a translator. Sometimes his doctors tease him, especially before they diagnose his illness as a severe brain infection. "The physician caring for me [now]," he complains, "knew my story, and he would laugh at the minute descriptions of symptoms that I furnished him. A case of nerves, always nerves! The imagination of a hypochondriac, of a literary person!" And so long as he is considered a malingerer ("the clearest case of a psychosomatic") his minute descriptions of symptoms do little more than annoy the doctors. The lesser doctors see them as irrelevant fabrications of a fictionalizing mind, especially before an accurate diagnosis has been made. After Dr. Foster Kennedy (one of the heroes of the book) has made his accurate diagnosis, the patient's account of signs and symptoms becomes more important, though not to every doctor. At the eye, ear, and nose clinic, for example, he is nothing more than his chart: "I was merely another hospital case. I had become an object of clinical curiosity, simply another bundle of humanity." He is asked nothing. He has no story to narrate, apparently, at least not one that will interest this "chief" of clinic. What interests this clinician is that he has a "case" before him, not a sentient human being who might have something worthwhile to say about what goes on in his body or who might offer precise descriptions of shifts in the location of pain and its changing effects. Instead, we are told, "this person grabbed me brusquely by the hair and began to describe my condition to the visitor. Pulling at my hair, he forced me to incline my head first to the right and then to the left. He pulled at my ears and looked into them. He peered into my eyes, nose, throat, all the while describing my symptoms, without the least caution or with any consideration for the person of the bearer. I did not exist. I was a sheaf of symptoms."

What has happened involves something beyond the narrator's

perception that his personality and identity carry little importance in this sort of field hospital, under battlefield conditions. It involves the all-too-effective stripping away of his one great weapon in the war that we all know as life: his powers of narration. Earlier one doctor had smilingly dismissed the validity of his account of his symptoms, but this one doesn't even allow him to tell his narrative. The effect of this is to marginalize him further, a descent into hell that began with his arrival at Bellevue Hospital on a snowy morning on the last day of November 1945. He describes his first hour in that high-ceilinged, dark, overheated place:

> I entered . . . alienated and crushed . . . like a man . . . who looks for and finds his last refuge. There was red tape—on and on. Finally, wearing the sorry garments of the hospitalized and wrapped in a blanket, I was wheeled to an elevator, and after many turns I arrived at the men's neurological ward. . . . The doctor helped me into bed, and my wife, trying all the while to appear unworried, left to attend to some problem or other. I was on my own, lost somewhat in that other world which suddenly seemed to be the only one on which I could still make a claim.

This first recognition that this utterly different world is now the only one that has a place for him will be confirmed and reconfirmed as over the next few days he sinks deeper and deeper into thinking about his plight. He carefully scans his fellow patients, seeing them as both individuals and types, but this survey serves only to sink him further into the sick role he has so eagerly assumed. Of some forty patients on the neurological ward, he singles out four. The first one is comatose. His physician seems bent only on screaming him into consciousness. A second patient, on the narrator's left, is a young, light-skinned black who, having been knifed in a fight, is partly paralyzed. Because of his extensive experience in the infirmary, he is able to convince the narrator right off that he is in for surgery. After all, the narrator's placement has significance: " 'This row of beds is reserved for surgical cases,' he said, with the same emphasis and peculiar relish sick people use in pronouncing words that are scientific and unusual." The third patient is almost entirely paralyzed. He is described as one who yells for the bedpan always at the last moment with the discomfiting result that "the stench filled the air." The fourth one is described as a pale lad whose staring eyes provoke the narrator into questions: "Was he searching, perhaps, for a look of sympathy? Was he telling me that he was pitiable and lonely? Or was he trying to make me feel that we shared a common fate?" "I don't know," decides the narrator. But one message has come through. "What was certain in his look, I understood, was that we belonged to the same world, that world of the outsider and the condemned. That perception gave me my first moment of mental agony. Tears welled up in my eyes. It was not long before I convinced myself that it was all over for me." He is now certain that his disease has advanced beyond the possibility of effective treatment. He will die.

> Then, my eyes glassed over by bitter tears, through which I could hardly see the pallid countenance of my silent interlocutor in the row across from me, I asked for It to come, swiftly, silently, benevolently, and to gather me up restfully in its cold and wormy arms.
> It was at that instant, I can well swear to it, that I passed resolutely beyond the invisible frontier that separates the living from the dead. I faced the darkness, and with love and conviction, moved toward it. My eyes dried up almost immediately. I felt serene.
> The pallid boy continued to stare at me. I smiled at him kindly. Now I too belonged to his world, the world of men in transition.

Ultimately it is not the narrator's fate to cross the river of death into that undiscovered country. The screens go up all around him and the dead are removed from the ward, but he does not die. Death belongs instead to the pale lad, the messenger of death whose message the narrator at first heeds but later is able to reject with the aid of good medical care, of course, and massive doses of penicillin.

Still, there is something more beyond good professional care and the salubrious effects of employing Dr. Fleming's great discovery that enhances the author's recovery, that turns his mind and face away from the great death that beckons him. The patient, having resigned himself to the fact that he is about to die, is allowed—encouraged actually—to give an account of his symptoms and to describe his medical situation from his point of view. A Viennese physician asks him if he minds his bringing around his students of neurology to examine his "case." The patient agrees, partly in the spirit of cooperation, partly out of the vanity he likens to that of beggars "who scrupulously cultivate their running sores." The doctor goes through some familiar steps and says the usual things—" '*Pontine angle*' . . ." and so forth, with the patient silently praying: "But, for God's sake, do not shake the bed. It rattles my brains." Then, to the narrator's surprise, the physician turns to him and asks him to describe his symptoms—to "narrate the history of my case." And what is the reaction of this man who has had his prior accounts of his illness cut off, ridiculed, dismissed? "I jumped at the chance and told my story with the relish and precision native to a hypochondriac." He has not only been asked to tell his story, he has been encouraged to narrate a tale at the end of which the physician will turn to his students and comment: " 'Rarely can a patient give us such a clear, subjective description of his condition. Such a thing calls for powers of sharp observation and an uncommon ability at expression. Only a physician can do it—or a writer. *Ziz iz fery, fery imporrtant!* For example . . .' "

The Viennese physician goes on to narrate an exemplary tale, which carries its own importance. But before reproducing it here we should be certain that we take full cognizance of what has just transpired. The physician has validated the patient's narration of his own medical situation by insisting that only a medical doctor or a writer could offer such a lucid, subjective narration. In short, description and history preceding diagnosis, the narratives of the doctor and the writer are judged to be similarly valuable. What this means to the narrator of *A Man Smiles at Death*, whose imagination has heretofore been linked to malingering, cannot be overstressed. The attention accorded his narrative will determine the way he will henceforth see himself.

But first, here is the Viennese doctor's own tale, as the patient-narrator tells it indirectly:

> [He] told the story of a Viennese cardiologist who himself suffered from a case of incurable heart disease. At death's very door (and working by himself) he had inserted the probe of a registering device among his arteries and into one of the cavities in his heart. Seated before the device, watching the needle trace on a drum the graph of his drawn-out agony, he expired. They found him at his work table, face-down, pen in hand, his last word broken off . . . A hero and a martyr to Science!

At this point, having concluded his narration to the smiling approval of his students, the doctor turns to the patient and asks him about his racket. "I told him what I did, how I earned my living, and that by vocation I was (woe be it to me) a frustrated, unfulfilled writer," he answers. " 'Didn't I tell you?' counter[s] the physician, flush with perspicacity."

But significant as this little parable of the importance of narrative to doctor and writer alike appears to be to Miguéis' book, it does not conclude the scene. The Viennese doctor has not brought the patient good news about his condition. He is not the bearer of an encouraging prognosis, which might well have colored the patient's reaction to the incident. On the contrary. The physician, pleased that under questioning his students have come up with an accurate diagnosis (having been skillfully led to it, the narrator tells us, by his own account), now concludes his lesson on this dire note:

" 'Cases like this are extremely rare, and hardly ever do they get to us *alive*. Frankly, this is the first one I have seen. Just a few days ago I performed an autopsy on an identical case—a great involvement in the cerebellum of the first, second, third par, and all the way down. *Total* devastation of the central nervous system!' "

The narrator, not silenced by this grim concluding note, fires back: " 'I am much obliged for your encouraging prognosis!' " Everyone around the bed laughs, the patient among them. Miguéis ends this chapter with a summing up of what the episode has meant for the patient-narrator:

> They had turned me into a guinea pig. Theirs and mine. There I was, watching myself suffer as if I were somebody else. Despite the Master's (Kennedy's) extreme discretion, I had learned a great deal lying there on my sick bed. But now nothing could upset me. I was ready to win. I wanted to help them win this battle.
>
> I had learned a great deal, and had had some fun, too.

The man who has already seen himself as one of those marked for death and therefore alienated from the living beings whose consciousness is not dominated by thoughts of the angel of death now shows no bitterness at his having become merely the object of his doctors' clinical experiments. He has made a discovery and it has transformed him. It has been revealed to him that he can become the object of an experiment of his own. In short, even at this late stage of what might well be a final illness he begins to function as an engaged narrator-observer. And not only is he capable of so doing, but, miracle of miracles, he has been called upon to do so by a physician. In fact, it takes no ingenuity to formulate the next identification: the doctor's observations are to his diagnosis what the writer's observations are to his narrative. After all, are not doctor and writer both narrators, each telling and retelling narratives that turn pain into myth?

A MAN SMILES
AT DEATH
WITH
HALF A FACE

Author's Preface

While sketching out these pages devoted to memories of a critical illness, among so many pages that perhaps some day I will collect into a larger volume, I came up against a problem. Up to what point can a writer talk about his personal experiences, without incurring the opprobrious label of subjectivism and without being indiscreet about himself? Is it possible in this day and age and in a milieu like ours, which is traditionally contrary and prejudiced against the confessional literature that has enriched and helped to clarify so many other cultures, to employ the frankness of Rousseau, Stendhal, Bashkirtseva, not to mention De Quincey or Baudelaire? Flaubert left us our first documentary account of epilepsy, one which gives us so much to think about in the case of the Jean-Jacques of the *Confessions*. James Joyce's biographers go to great lengths to describe his blindness and his gastric ulcer. And what about Uriel da Costa? Scott Fitzgerald? And to go to the extreme of indiscretion, consider how much has been speculated on Camilo's "necrophilia" and Júlio Dinis' chastity. It has even been "explained" that Antero's anguish resulted from pressure of the pylorus or cardia, I don't really know which, and his suicide—my heavens!—as the result of an increase in the atmospheric pressure. Suffering as part of the fabric of existence is an enigma that engages mankind.

But independently of such disproportion as exists among these cases, the question is moot from the start, for it is not essentially the author we are dealing with here, but rather that which, in the author's personal experience, might be common, communicable, even useful, as example and lesson, to other men. This is not an egotistical confession, not the confession of secret acts and thoughts, nor even the sounding of an "odious I," but a human case narrated at first hand by its closest witness with the objectivity of a novel, and with the purpose of stirring up certain general problems such as those surrounding the perturbations of illness and death, and the individual's attitudes toward physical suffering and personal destiny.

Yes, it was first of all, for hypochondriacs—those people frightened of sickness and obsessed with termination —that I wrote these pages in my journal; later, for those who want to know the reactions of someone lying in a hospital bed, surrounded by death; and then, perhaps, for those physicians interested in knowing how their patients view them.

I tried to paint a real ambience, that of the hospital in a great modern metropolis, where pain and brutality, sweetness and humor, and, in particular, devotion by physician and nurse, give it the features of tragedy and epic, before which the personal case is erased and vanishes.

What writer, having at his disposal such material from lived-through experience, would refuse to treat it objectively, painting the scenes and characters of a drama that daily plays itself out at his bedside but which remains unknown, forgotten, or shrouded prejudicially in modesty? After all, do not people write memoirs of war, dungeons, and concentration camps? Might it not be healthy to show as well the mud through which man drags himself and into which he is sometimes immersed so that he might emerge from it and thus purified free himself from it?

What matters to the writer—the subjectivizer of the objective, the interpreter of the reactions of the individual before the calamities that threaten him from all sides—is that he recreate for his readers a picture of the experience of which he was the center, thereby giving them the illusion, instructive perhaps, of being themselves the actors in a drama.

If, in sketching some of these episodes I have sprinkled them here and there with a bit of irony, I have done so always with the emotion-filled gratitude and the deepest respect for those authen-

tic apostles of medicine that I have known. We—all human beings—
make mistakes, and we should not expect that men in white will
not make them. Not by any stretch of the imagination have I ever
been tempted to engage in the satire that for millennia has targeted
doctors. One can say of them as has been said of women and Jews,
they may be pelted by epigrams and under attack, but humanity
would not know how to live, nor could it live, without them.

J.R.M.

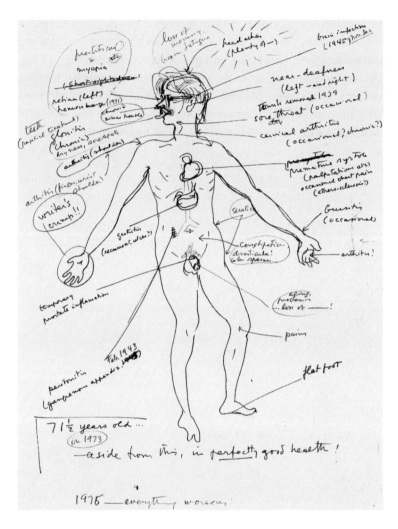

Miguéis as hypochondriac and patient—a self-portrait done in 1973. Courtesy of John Hay Library, Brown University.

I

I awoke at three A.M., in a cold sweat, twisting and turning with cramps. I took a sedative and waited. The pain got worse, and my wife, alarmed, telephoned the doctor. "Don't worry," he responded in a sleepy, tired voice. "There's nothing seriously wrong with your husband. Give him some strong coffee and another sedative."

This same practitioner, whom I was seeing in the absence of my own physician, Dr. Milton Kissin, then on military service in India, had recently said to me as I stood before the X-ray screen: "You are suffering merely from spasms of the colon. Look, here you have the image of a typical spastic colon. It's a bit of nerves and, let's face it, a touch of hypochondria."

I had long ago become used to physical pain. For many years I had suffered from gastrointestinal indisposition—the so-called centrointestine mucomembraneosis (colitis) then so much in vogue—and I suffered frequent attacks of catarrh in the sinuses which tied me to my bed for days at a time, unable to work, to move my head, or even tolerate sunlight. In Brussels once I got up from a sickbed to take an examination, and shut up by myself in an amphitheater at the medical school and waiting to be called, with my head in my arms, I heard echoing in the room my own voice answering questions. I realized that I was delirious and fell silent. Dr. Péchère, a teacher of Social and Scholastic Hygiene, became wary of my demeanor during the examination and offered to see me in his office in a few days. His office was in a splendid modern building close by the Étangs de Ixelles. After a lengthy examination, which included various tests for "stamina," he declared, shaking his venerable head, "To be candid, I cannot see, given your condition, how it is that you are still among the living, let alone working!" That was in 1930 or '31. It seemed like a death sentence. I laughed. And to this day, after all these struggles, attacks, and ambushes, I still laugh. There exists in man an incommensurable power of resistance.

The years went by. I remained active and happy, as well as no stranger to polemics or even merely a good fight, never retreating before a moral risk—a bundle of nerves vibrating within a carcass of skin and bones; but being divided among preoccupations over ideas and literature and over earning a living and keeping physically active, I perhaps devoted too much attention to the multiple ills that besieged me, even though, since succumbing to that unfailing "second-childhood" disease measles, I had never had any serious illness. (Or so I thought, even though at the age of twelve or thirteen, I had gone through a period of atrocious stomach pains.)

Then was I really a hypochondriac? And did I have good reason to be one? To what extent had I been so affected by chronic sinusitis that it brought about in me an excessive sensitivity to illness and the jitters, I could not say. I even got to the point of laughing at myself, saying, *"Nulla dies sine dolore!"* (There is no such thing as a day without pain.) There are those who claim that certain respiratory diseases are common to nervous types. That is like asking what came first, the chicken or the egg. Man is a unitary being, and it is always by way of the body, and in the body, that he suffers. Are we not beginning to penetrate the mysterious realm of cellular physical-chemistry which might give us, among other things, the key to mental illness? Psychic activity offers life its most subtle relationship between the two worlds of man and things. It is not surprising, then, that man's body should reflect his conflicts and clashes.

Meanwhile, I would give the doctors minute descriptions of my symptoms, a thing that can perplex them, and which some-times sets them against the patient, but which, in every case, puts them on the defensive. After all, the clinician is a man, and his power is limited. We ask so much of him, we ascribe to him so much responsibility, expecting from his still circumscribed science and art cures for all illnesses, including those that are not seldom imaginary. Sedatives and antispasmodics were prescribed. Dr. Milton Kissin, my friend and helper, and a clinician of exceeding knowledge and honesty, would say to me, "To feel bad is not necessarily to be ill, and to feel good is not always equivalent to being healthy. Certain individuals have an uncommonly low threshold for pain, and at the slightest stimulus suffer excessively. If fear of illness does not generate illness, unfortunately neither does it prevent it or cure it."

In his opinion and that of other physicians, I was, in fine, what is called a "functional sick man" or, in more modern terms, a "psychosomatic." I would settle for that—with my sinusitis, gastrointestinal episodes, emaciation and diffuse pains—and go on living an active life with the hope for better days. I did not turn away from heavily spiced food or give up nights spent in discussion and conversation conducted amid cigarette smoke and a few fortifying drinks. On one occasion I did manage to get the doctors to extract my tonsils, long since infected, and my condition improved a bit. (When I was a boy, there was an affable Navy doctor working in a Lisbon clinic who over several months tried to rid my tonsils of the abundant colonies of crypt-dwellers that inhabited their numerous cavities, without obtaining any result other than that of giving me pain and making me bleed. But he would not operate.)

At the time I was forty-two, but felt ten years younger and lived as if I were actually no more than thirty-two. It never crossed my mind that I might be entering into a general decline. I worked intensively, had friends, love, a daughter. And after a few years of conflicts and difficulties that resulted in a nervous attack (about which I shall not at this time speak; I'm saving that for a more propitious occasion), I had a routine, more or less, which I followed in my spare time and during Saturdays, Sundays, and evenings, to fill reams of paper with the unpublishable prose of a Portuguese writer *in partibus infidelium*. It was my way of continuing to live my life in Portugal, without actually being there. (Faced with the failure of my few efforts to be read in English, I convinced myself early on that it was preferable to remain Portuguese, even if that meant I would remain unpublished.) That winter of 1943–44, therefore, was very hard. My sinusitis, which had dried up, now once again became active, and bronchitis prostrated me. I lived in a state of excessive mental tension with all my defenses enfeebled. I weighed a mere 54 kilos—20 kilos less than, theoretically, I should weigh. That was when it all came to a crisis.

As time went on the pain got worse. I was sweating and moaning. At my wife's urging, Dr. X finally promised to come to see me. But, fatigued, he fell asleep in his tub (at the risk of drowning) and did not show up until around seven. It was wartime. Doctors were scarce, and each one of them did the work of ten. An old and pleasant surgeon, my landlord and neighbor, Dr. Coccuzza, had come up to see me and, displeased, said, "It doesn't seem like appendicitis to me." On leaving he looked back, "Still, to be on the safe side, I'd open him up—his abdomen. Who knows?"

By the time Dr. X finally arrived I was exhausted. I can still remember his cold hands as they poked around over my tense and aching abdomen. Conclusion. It was not appendicitis. Then what was it? I insisted on being taken to Beth Israel Hospital, just a few steps away, where I had had my tonsils extracted. "Don't even think about it!" he said. "There isn't a room available, and they won't accept you without my saying so!"

"We'll see about that!" said I. I got out of bed, dressed, descended five flights of stairs (I always lived in old houses with no elevators, those brownstones that are giving way to progress), crossed the park at an angle and limped into the hospital, all the while with a knife tearing away at my insides. I was given a room and put to bed. They took my blood, urine, secretions, and temperature. They touched me and poked me, rapped me and tapped me all over. They debated over me in their profession's unintelligible argot. It was not appendicitis! I was suffering, but I was also amused. On seeing the rose-colored discharge that came from my nose when I blew it, Dr. X exclaimed triumphantly, "You see! That's what's making him suffer!"

They gave me analgesics, I presume. The pain abated a little and I, weak and perplexed, calmed down.

Toward late afternoon, while talking with a friend, I was hit by a fit of intermittent fevers. My teeth were knocking like castanets and I lost the ability to speak. When the attack was over, though I was conscious and lucid, I began to react less to the people and the happenings around me. I sank into a strange quiescence and beatitude. Even my pain seemed to be impersonal and off at a distance. I looked into a small mirror and saw a denuded and pallid face, a slender nose. Where had I seen the like? The distant memory of a loved one—my dead brother—gave me the chills. I thought: "I have the face of a dying man. What will they do? Why don't they do something?"

The doctors came by frequently. In the dead of night and in my torpor, I heard the muffled voice of the surgeon, Dr. Isaacs, harshly scolding my wife, who had resolved to spend the night at my side, curled up in a small armchair. "What, madame, are you doing here? Do you want to spoil your husband rotten? Go home. Right now!"

(She had helped me so many times during other illnesses—always solicitous and sympathetic, suffering because she saw me suffering, running the risk of babying me!)

Dr. Isaacs enjoyed a reputation for rudeness and was on the outs with many of that hospital's doctors, including my current attending physician. But it was everyone's opinion that he was highly competent. Perceiving that he was being discourteous, I fantasized that I raised myself from the pillow to hit him with a couple of hard truths—that that was no way to treat my vexed wife. But I did not move at all or utter a single word. It was as if everything was taking place behind a thick crystal plate. I was losing contact with reality and sinking into drowsiness and unconsciousness. And I knew it.

Early the next morning I awoke to a great hullabaloo. The doctors again congregated, talking their Molièresque language. In my torpor I understood only their conclusion. I would be operated on—"an emergency"—twenty-four hours late. I smiled at my wife and murmured, "At last." My smile was probably imbecilic. But inside I knew what I wanted. I wanted to escape that apathy, confront the test, confirm what was wrong with me, save myself, live.

With a thousand precautions they transferred me to the stretcher, all done aseptically. There was a certain comfort in all of that. In the corridor I glanced at the large electric clock hanging from the ceiling. It was ten on the dot. "How long will this take?" It was then (I found out later) that my wife, in distress, demanded that the doctor explain my condition. "It could be almost anything," he said, which was the same thing as saying, "get ready for the worst!" Was he thinking about cancer?

I was given a spinal anesthetic. On the operating table, with my eyes covered over, I could hear and feel everything, except pain. I remained attentive to the curt and muffled voices within the masks, to the tense and charged atmosphere in the operating room, to the painless incision, to the hands that were handling my viscera, to the pull of the catgut, to the tinkling of the instruments. A dear friend, the Brazilian neurosurgeon Nilson de Rezende, assisted in the operation. He gave my right hand a squeeze and whispered into my ear, "Everything is going well. Take heart!" I was moved by that and it made me happy. In times of stress all signs of affection become greatly magnified.

There was as yet no such thing as penicillin. Before closing up the incision they powdered me with sulfa drugs.

While being wheeled back to my room I remembered the ceiling clock and uncovered my face. It read a quarter to eleven. The time had flown! I was consoled and felt light as a cloud, but extremely weak and inert.

In the final analysis, it turned out, I had a case of extensive peritonitis. My appendix, gangrenous and purulent, showed itself encysted in the caecum. It bore a scar from a prior infection, which must have healed spontaneously under the auspices of my "hypochondria" and my "spastic attacks." All this, they told me, had made it difficult to locate it by touch and to make a diagnosis. Had my "hypochondria" blinded them to the signs of an organic malfunction? I don't know. What did it matter now? The "expression of anxiety" to which the secret report made reference at the time of my admittance and which had so perturbed Dr. X was fully justified. But I did not feel spite or acrimony toward the doctor. On the contrary, I considered myself free from the threat that had so long kept me from living peacefully. When shortly thereafter he appeared before me, pale with fatigue and sleeplessness, I told him, "Well, doctor, I expect that this will put an end to *our* nervous spasms!"

We both smiled, relieved.

The shock was profound, the crisis dragged on, and for a long time I was on the danger list.

The first few days they fed me intravenously. Things looked distant and nebulous. Smells made me nauseous. I had to beg a middle-aged nurse not to come near me mornings after she had sprayed herself with the inexpensive cologne she could afford to buy. I found its peculiar odor intolerable.

She must have been insulted, but I had no choice. The very paper handkerchiefs—facial tissues—sent waves of nausea through me. My abdomen, veritably a sack of stones, was in painful stasis. I developed gastritis and couldn't even swallow saliva without groaning in pain. I was hit with another inflammatory complication which is hardly worth mentioning. How long would the test last? I prepared myself to wait. I saw myself surrounded by dear friends, medical attention, solicitous nursing, and, despite the suffering, I felt pacified and happy—as if I were resting at the bottom of a well of warmth and gentleness. The long incision healed with astonishing rapidity.

The days went by slowly. The telephone brought into my insular hospital room the tumult of the life outside—we were at war and I was in that place! During the long nights the fierce February winds shook the steel window frames, the overcast sky showed all the congested reflections of the monstrous city, the hot breath of the radiators reached my bed, and in that strange quiet and penumbra of the corridor where a nurse, sitting at a small table, read and studied under light from a green lampshade, I could hear the breathing and moaning of other patients, who would sometimes cry out in the horror of worry or as the result of anesthesia, and I listened to muffled murmurs, and quick, light steps. Down there, by the window, I could see the immense illumination of a movie-house sign—"The Academy of Music"—whose lights ran interminably one after the other like a string of small goldfish chasing themselves. In all this there was something comforting that cannot be put into words.

Even though I knew that I was being attended to day and night, each morning I impatiently awaited my private-duty nurse, Miss Goldis. At eight, on the dot, she would throw open the shutters, smile, and with a voice that was a bird's warbling and which brought me a breath of active, healthy life, bid me "Good morning!" She would give me a sponge bath while I was in bed, rub me with alcohol, change my sheets every day (from her I learned how to make a bed with a patient in it), serve me breakfast, converse with me, and laugh with me to get my mind off my troubles. Afterward, snug in my remade bed and lulled by her cheerful, gentle voice, I would nap, hearing only vaguely the hospital's morning noises, the whirr of the floor-waxers in the corridors. She would then tiptoe out of the room or sit down quietly to read. She would stay with me until 4 P.M., talk to me about the ballet, which she was studying, about books, about her friends, and her plans for the future.

Was all this attention merely a function of her professional technique or was it sincerely cordial? Whatever it was, I blessed her, marveled at her patience, good humor, efficiency, and hard work. (For some years afterward, whenever we ran into each other, we behaved like two old friends and confidants. I only hope that somewhere Miss Goldis is now doing what she always wanted to do—teaching art in some high school.)

Even during my hours of solitude and quiet, the idea of death never occurred to me, an idea that seemed to obsess me in so many of my stories and which (I thought) explained my maniacal fear of illness. Was I really a hypochondriac, as they had led me to believe? In that hospital room I did a lot of thinking.

What is a hypochondriac? Does an obsession with illness express a fear of death or an exaggerated attachment to life? Is hypochondria a defense mechanism for those who, fearing their demise, search out vivid ways to shield themselves from the threat? Or is it a defense, like that of children who, playing at war, crime, horrors, and deaths, expose themselves to risks that could destroy them? Or, contrariwise, is hypochondria the dramatization of the subjective gratification of an obscure desire for annihilation? Can it be the expression of the feeling of guilt, as the pure Freudians have it, a form of self-punishment or "castration"? Or, rather, is hypochondria a way of evading the responsibilities and exigencies of our everyday social lives? A loophole for the indolent and timid, for those who entrench themselves behind walls of symptoms so that they can tell the world: "Ah, see what I would be capable of doing if I only had my health. Don't ask me for anything or expect anything of me. I am a sick man. Count me out"? Can it be that the hypochondriac is a kind of unrecognized masochist who lives by fantasizing flagellations for which he sighs (of which he fakes fear and dare not ask for) so that later he can confront the culminating moment of danger and trespass with the stoic's serenity and the saint's jubilation?

The fear of death is worse than death itself, and that is why so many combatants, out of control and hallucinated, leap from the trenches and shelters and run toward the enemy's lines, in search of death.

But what do we know—layman or expert—of the thousand obscure tendencies that ensnare us? The best authorities disagree. To seek out answers to these questions is like trying to explain what a dream is and the reasons for our dreaming; or what esthetic creation is, and to what end we create; or what love is, and why we do not merely submit to satisfying our biological impulse to preserve the species, but have thrown ourselves, over millennia, into so many ecstasies, deliriums, and tragedies of passion. We have made so many marvelous discoveries in these areas without, however, having come to an accepted universal conclusion, or, what is more, one that is always therapeutically productive. There is still so much we do not know about ourselves.

In the meantime, there I was, enjoined in combat with that "combination of forces that oppose themselves to life"—to paraphrase (in reverse) old Le Dantec. Was I too trusting? Insensible? Dormant?

I remember that, closing my eyes, I dreamt I was somewhere amidst rocks, naked and hot in the sun, bathing in the *bassin* of cool water cascading over me. This fantasy, which repeated itself numerous times, cooled me and invigorated me. I also went for long imaginary walks, planned trips and excursions that unfortunately to this day have not been taken. So many times during the month I spent there, I walked the mountains of Arrábida in the company of a dear Brazilian friend who had hoped to come to Portugal in his country's service; and we would end up in Setubal in a *casa de pasto*, an "eating-house" (please excuse my plebeian archaism) close by the quays. We would eat surmullets (broiled in butter), with parsley and lime. Dare I recommend this therapy through fantasy to those beings confined to beds?

My recovery picked up speed. One night I got up by myself,

against my nurse's advice, and without any heed for my "adhesions." Dr. Isaacs, who used to look in frequently, gave me a friendly tap on the arm and said, "You're a good patient. I like you." His pleasure was evident. I must confess that, his rough exterior notwithstanding, I reciprocated sympathetically. I have always liked "aggressive" people who speak their minds (in contrast, perhaps, to my own ancient reserve and timidity), and above all when they are doctors, for I understand that frankness and severity itself can be exceptionally helpful in treatment. Most patients want to be coddled, to have their innumerable symptoms flattered, to be given bundles of prescriptions from the clinician's hands, even when no medicine is required. A woman friend, a university person besieged by obstacles, went to a physician to complain of several ailments that she did not have. He examined her, found her to be, for her seventy years and more, fit as a fiddle, and prescribed nothing. "Would you mind if I took a little oil of ricinus?" she asked him angrily, and never went back. The doctor laughed as he told me about her. "Perhaps eighty percent of the patients who enter this office have nothing wrong with them, unless it's fear, or the desire to have some illness," he said. "And all they want is the doctor's complicity, sympathy, and consoling words. But these people help me get a living! Most of them are disappointed when we fail to discover that at the least they have cancer. And those who momentarily feel relieved of their vexation waste little time in inventing another one. At this very moment your friend is probably in the hands of one of my less experienced or less scrupulous colleagues." Like the frightened fallen horse, mortals need doctors to pull on their reins, put the spurs to them, and get them to sniff out the shadows that are the source of their fright.

Dr. Isaacs, after all, had saved my life. I could not help feeling grateful. And I am certain that I was grateful not merely for his having opened up my abdomen.

When in March, after a month, I returned home and was carried up the stairs by my brothers-in-law, I saw in myself a new man, one who was liberated for all time from his "spastic colon" and some other little ailments. (Indeed, for a long time afterward I had no digestive problems as I had had up till then, and a great deal of my nervousness did disappear.) The first thing I did, the minute I was alone, was to remake my bed the way Miss Goldis taught me.

I went back to work. I spent a good two months taking care of a painful complication; for some time I had an intolerable skin itch (probably caused by the sulfa drugs), but I soon got back my color, appetite, vigor, and confidence. And even my weight went up some. I felt capable of making new efforts and taking on new tasks.

"Hypochondriac!" I would say, voluptuously pulling out my abdominal stitches, one by one. "I'll give you 'psychosomatic!'"

But my difficulties were far from over.

II

My sinusitis continued to flare up at times, but nothing like before, and I didn't pay much attention to it. That condition was already systemic to my life and part of the picture. I smoked much too much, given my condition, but kept putting off the day (as I still do) when courageously or out of fear I would give up smoking. I felt congested, all blocked up, had persistent headaches, a rare thing for me, and my stuffed-up nose seemed to have stopped functioning. I now frequently used "nose drops," which helped me to breathe again. I had a constant need for pure, cold air and would go out winter nights, into the snow, to get relief.

In the fall of 1945, a year and a half after my bout with peritonitis, I began to suffer from strange perturbations. One night I awoke with a start. There was a hammering sensation in my head. I fell into an agitated sleep. I didn't have the mental and physical energy of times past. Maybe it was age. I was working very hard, and now I was happily, if imprudently, embarked on new and risky ventures. Little by little, a steel ring tightened around my head. Something had happened to my eyesight and I could no longer see at all well through my customary lenses. The ophthalmologist noticed that I had a slight strabismus and wrote me a stronger prescription. I was feeling slightly muddleheaded and was seized by an inexplicable distress that seemed to narrow my physical and mental horizons. The physician caring for me during Dr. Milton Kissin's absence knew my story, and he would laugh at the minute descriptions of symptoms that I furnished him. A case of nerves, always nerves! The imagination of a hypochondriac, of a literary person! The clearest case of a psychosomatic.

It seemed natural to me, given my temperament and my habit of self-analysis, that every small symptom would exaggerate itself. The man must be right. He was a good young clinician, and I had confidence in him. Headaches? Aspirin. Irritability? Anxiety? Phenobarbital. I became, temporarily, a pill-taker. Everybody I knew took pills. I took them too, though with moderation. I took a lot of vitamins, B complex. And I used to put drops into my nose to reduce congestion so that I could breathe. "You'll make it to ninety," he would tell me, optimistically and encouragingly.

Then I noticed that telephone voices were becoming intolerable, causing me sharp pain in my inner left ear. I started to use my right ear for listening, which was not habitual with me. The irritability increased. My vision became distorted and I had difficulty focusing. It was like looking through flawed glass or water. I lived in the anticipation that something was going to happen to me. But what?

One rainy day in November, when it was already dark out, I returned home in distress. I had a headache and a slight fever. I called the doctor, who came the following morning. I had gone to see him two days earlier and had asked him to give me penicillin.

Now he found me in bed. He smiled and said, "Well, did it take merely a visit to the doctor to make you sick?" But he was intrigued and prescribed penicillin inhalations, through an atomizer.

It was much too late. The pain in the left hemisphere of my brain intensified. Each pulsation was a stab. My sensitivity to sound became so acute that a pin hitting the floor was enough to startle me and give me a sharp pain. In my head I heard the insufferable whirring of telegraph wires and the chirping of birds. My muddle increased, my eyes palpitated in spasms, my walk turned into a stagger. And that running fever persisted.

Then one morning, as I was brushing my teeth, I noticed that the water was running out of the left side of my mouth, as if from a torn sack. My upper lip drooped inertly to the left, and I was no longer able to shape my lips as if to whistle. It was a stroke. My facial paralysis spread quickly, and I was sure I was doomed. There was something abnormal going on in my brain. I rushed to the doctor, who became noticeably anxious. He gave me a quick neurological examination and sent me immediately to the radiologist.

Lucky for me, that same day my friend Nilson de Rezende arrived from Washington and came to visit me. (Had my wife called him?) When he saw me he became apprehensive. Alleging that I had a case of Bell's paralysis ("a children's thing") so as not to alarm me, he arranged for Professor Foster Kennedy, whose assistant he had once been, to see me without delay. I would have had to wait two weeks, otherwise, which would have made it all too late.

I went to see Dr. Kennedy that very afternoon. The examination lasted nearly two hours. It was not "Bell's palsy." In conclusion, with only the two of us present in his spacious office, sitting before a fireplace in which burned a fake-wood electrical fire, the great neurologist spoke to me precisely and gravely:

"I don't want to mislead you into believing that you are suffering from a cerebral tumor. But quite possibly you have an abscess, and most certainly a grave infection in a very delicate area of the encephalon." He put his finger firmly to the base of my skull and added: "Here! Lucky for you it is a facial paralysis. If not for that, even I might not be able to help you. Your condition, to speak frankly, is grave. I want you admitted to the hospital this very day, so that we can begin treatment tomorrow morning. There's no time to lose."

In my lamentable neurological confusion, but with concentrated fervor, I listened to him. I drank in the magisterial words that came from his mouth and which might be announcing my irrevocable death sentence but which also, given his authority, offered hope and the promise of a cure. Foster Kennedy was one of the most expensive and most exclusive physicians in the Empire City. Poor man of letters that I was and translator by trade, I could never have become his private patient. "My fee," he said, "would devour your meager savings. Would you mind the infirmary at Bellevue Hospital? It would be a curious experience for a writer." Led by him, I would have descended into Hell itself.

But not then, not that afternoon of intense cold and mounting snowfall, would I go into the hospital. Alleging that I had things that urgently needed doing, that I had to put my life in order and I know not what else, I put off going to the hospital until the next morning. To what hope and confidence was I entrusting myself? Upon returning home, reeling and feverish, I rushed to read everything I possessed regarding the normal and pathological ways of the cerebellum. I learned (and re-remembered) many frightening things. Then, by myself, I repeated some of the neurological tests that the Master and his assistant had given me. I experienced the illusion that I was already getting better, and that I could almost keep my balance, eyes shut, without falling off to the left. Such is the will's strength, even in a "hypochondriac." But I could not whistle, close my left eye, stand on my left leg, or walk a straight line.

This implacable infection encircled my head, putting my life in danger. But my brain, even though shot through by darts of pain at each pulsation of blood, was active and functioning. That night, which despite a dozen aspirin was one of insomnia, I conceived a story that seemed to have nothing to do with illness and death. It was about an expatriate who returns to Portugal after an absence of twenty years and tries to re-establish himself.*

In that story I was trying to give expression, perhaps, to my hope and desire to live, to return to my people, to participate in their lives and live among them, to satisfy that organic (and imperious) necessity to write about and for those others—not for and about myself alone. For years now, my unpublished book had been wandering around Brazil, like a lost son.

The next morning I had great difficulty walking. I felt weak, and I walked with legs opened wide and feet turned out, like Demoor's dog with a mutilated brain. The pain was piercing. All noises, as well as my deafness, were aggravated. Eye spasms frenzied my vision. My bewilderment was intolerable. In front of me the world pulsed and oscillated, almost unrecognizably.

Meanwhile, that November's early snow accumulated, piled high by Canadian winds. The city was laid out in white with a spectral silence. My wife had gone for a taxi, but at some distance it had gotten stuck in the middle of the street. The street itself was obstructed by still-soft snow in high and low mounds that I had to cross as if they were dunes of loose sand, staggering and sliding like a falling, pained, moaning drunk. To me the snow, which ordinarily I loved, was like a tomb. My solitude became infinite, like that of a person condemned to deportation to the moon. I

---

*The story "Simbólico, na Cúpula da Pena," first published in December 1947 in the journal *Ver e Crer*, was later collected as "Regresso à Cúpula da Pena" in *Léah e Outras Histórias* (Estúdios Cor: Lisbon, 1958). [As "Return to the Cupola," this story appears in English translation in the collection of Miguéis stories *Steerage and Ten Other Stories* (Providence, R.I.: Gávea-Brown, 1983).—*(Translator's note.)*].

thought I couldn't make it. Was this, sadly, how my expatriate wanderings would end?

I entered the immense, dark, and overheated Bellevue Hospital like a man alienated and crushed, who looks for and finds his last refuge. There was red tape—on and on. Finally, wearing the sorry garments of the hospitalized and wrapped in a blanket, I was wheeled to an elevator, and after many turns I arrived at the men's neurological ward.

There were no beds. They were short of nurses, medicine, auxiliaries, everything. "We are at war, sir. Do you understand?" I was told with asperity by the head nurse (or so I took her to be), who was irritated at the entré given me by Professor Kennedy's handwritten note when presented by my wife immediately upon our arrival. The note laconically informed the physician on duty: *"Angle point-cerebellum. First, second, third pair, etc. Penicillin.—F. K."* It referred to the pairs of affected cranial nerves. It said more than enough, even for a layman like me.

The infirmary was overflowing. The intern who received me, Dr. Bigby, finally got me a bed. Without paying attention to anyone, I sat down by the bed and rested my head—at the spot where the pain pulsed furiously—on my crossed arms. All I wanted was silence and immobility. An atrocious weight had begun to come down from my tormented head into my shoulders. The doctor helped me into bed, and my wife, trying all the while to appear unworried, left to attend to some problem or other. I was on my own, lost somewhat in that other world which suddenly seemed to be the only one on which I could still make a claim. It was then that I took my first look at my surroundings.

The atmosphere was not what one can call, strictly speaking, joyous. If the reader has ever found himself stuck in the vast infirmary ward of an old public hospital, it is most certain that he did not at all like the ambience, unless he was too beaten down at the time to notice anything at all. Well, I was perfectly lucid and therefore conscious of the strange, desolate, and fatiguing peace that follows the performance of early morning tasks in a hospital ward: the silence, indifference, the lonely curiosity, and even hostility with which the residents welcome the newcomer.

My surroundings were neither attractive nor encouraging, though they did serve to attenuate the optimism I had picked up at Beth Israel. Some forty men lay in beds somewhat crowded into this grayish, dark room with a very high ceiling, and they slept, waited, became delirious and overwrought, moaned and complained. Some ambulatory patients and convalescents were grouped about the immense windows at the far, eastern end of the room. They were reading newspapers, talking quietly, and playing cards. Others circulated randomly, dragging themselves along or being pushed about in wheelchairs, their eyes fixed vaguely on the bare greenish walls or on the distant ceiling decorated with shadows and spider webs. Some of them agonized in a chorus of labored breathing. Everything was dull and listless.

On my right, an enormous man, whose head was wrapped in bandages and who was tied to the bedsides, moaned and grunted unconsciously, moving convulsively from time to time. The physician who had operated on him, a young and attractive woman, would bend over him and cry out, imploringly: "Mister Hartman! Mister Hartman! Do you hear what I am saying to you?"

The man barked out from the depths of his misery—a sign that a ray of consciousness persisted in that half destroyed brain. She would persist: "Mister Hartman, answer me!"

On my left, a light-skinned Negro, still young, good-looking and well-spoken, started up a conversation. He told me he had been knifed in a Harlem dispute. Some nerves had been severed and he was now partly paralyzed. Having undergone several operations, he had acquired a good deal of experience in the ward. He knew its ways and customs. He told me immediately that I would be operated on. "This row of beds is reserved for surgical cases," he said, with the same emphasis and peculiar relish sick people use in pronouncing words that are scientific and unusual. I believed him and thought that out of pity they had decided to deceive me. I must have an abscess or tumor. But nothing, I thought, could exceed what I was already suffering. I was ready to agree with everyone and everything.

On the same side, over near the windows, a paralytic shouted for the nurse. She answered his cry for the bedpan, but arrived too late, and there was laughter around them. The stench filled the air.

My Negro companion smiled. He began reading magazines sporting naked women on their covers. An impotent man has to occupy his leisure moments doing something, don't you think? Mr. Hartman roared deafeningly into space and went into convulsions that threatened to snap ropes, boards, and bars. From the row of beds across from me, a young and pale boy stared sadly at me, as if he were listening for something or wanted to speak. Was he searching, perhaps, for a look of sympathy? Was he telling me that he was pitiable and lonely? Or was he trying to make me feel that we shared a common fate? I don't know. What was certain in his look, I understood, was that we belonged to the same world, that world of the outsider and the condemned. That perception gave me my first moment of mental agony. Tears welled up in my eyes.

It was not long before I convinced myself that it was all over for me. The Negro was right. They were going to operate. Abscess or tumor, the location of my illness in itself—at the base of the encephalon—marked me, by the difficulty it posed for the operation, to near-condemnation. And besides, we had waited too long. For much too much time the infection had spread silently, to the point where treatment (and which treatment?) would have no efficacy. That suppurating mass would pressure the central nervous center, spread to the bulb, and, like a fulminating poliomyelitis, annihilate me. Of "cerebral barriers" I knew enough to foresee that it would be difficult to use antibiotics. No one had yet had the courage to inject antibiotics directly to the cerebral cavities. Could it be done?

And even if they did save my life, I would be an asylum case, a paralytic tortured by spasms and pain, a physical and mental ruin, unable to see well, do battle, or work—an encumbrance serving only to aggravate my family's difficulties and vexations. I didn't want to live the larval existence of one who has to be tolerated, a dead weight, one worthy only of pity and to become its target. No. Rather death. Life is too good and too demanding for it to consent to the presence of such beings among those who battle, enjoy, and create. Not for nothing had I spent three years among abnormal beings in those institutions I attended as a student.

All my personal hopes, all those things that until then I had lived for—ideas, projects, work—were over, void, finished. The road descended before me, ever more narrow and deep, like a funnel going down into nothing, disappearing into the very ground's indifferent breast. No, I didn't want to live like that, not even for a minute. Better death. I wanted to die, and die I should! The sooner the better.

Then, my eyes glassed over by bitter tears, through which I could hardly see the pallid countenance of my silent interlocutor in the row across from me, I asked for It to come, swiftly, silently, benevolently, and to gather me up restfully in its cold and wormy arms.

It was at that instant, I can well swear to it, that I passed resolutely beyond the invisible frontier that separates the living from the dead. I faced the darkness, and with love and conviction, moved toward it. My eyes dried up almost immediately. I felt serene.

The pallid boy continued to stare at me. I smiled at him kindly. Now I too belonged to his world, the world of men in transition.

"The boss wants to know what the boys in nose and ears think of you," said Dr. Bigby. "We're going to the clinic."

I got up—cross, reeling from pain, and trembling with weakness—for still another test. They persisted in returning me to the world from which I had so gloriously broken away.

Then, I, who until that time had always been quick, well-balanced, and agile, sat down in the wheelchair, smothered in a blanket, and allowed the doctor to push me down the ward and through shadowy windswept corridors clogged with patients in beds, on stretchers, in wheelchairs, sitting on benches or just slowly wandering about. We went through other overflowing wards, amidst nauseating odors of cooking, disinfectants, and suppuration, and through moaning and crying. Dr. Bigby leaned over toward me and smiled, *"C'est la guerre!"*

It was, indeed, like a field hospital. We descended stairways, went down still other deserted corridors, and finally arrived at the ear, nose, and throat clinic. The intern delivered me into the hands of a nurse and disappeared. I remained in my wheelchair, my head heavy and oppressed with pain. I was nauseated. I waited a long time in that room, which was inhospitable and, by contrast with the others, freezing.

The chief of clinic (or so I supposed him to be)—a stout, florid man, just a bit over forty—was conversing animatedly with a visitor. He just forgot about me. I was now in the presence of strangers, who knew nothing about me, had no ties to me, and to whom I was merely another hospital case. I had become an object of clinical curiosity, simply another bundle of humanity.

After a quick look at the paperwork, this person grabbed me brusquely by the hair and began to describe my condition to the visitor. Pulling at my hair, he forced me to incline my head first to the right and then to the left. He pulled at my ears and looked into them. He peered into my eyes, nose, throat, all the while describing my symptoms, without the least caution or with any consideration for the person of the bearer. I did not exist. I was a sheaf of symptoms. I had symptoms to spare, however much that displeased me.

He diagnosed my nystagmus, and then, forcing me rudely to

bend my neck to the left, deposited some drops into my right ear to aggravate the painful phenomenon. They had a strong effect, for my ocular spasm became so accentuated and violent that I began to go crazy. In the midst of my intolerable bewilderment, the room was gyrating around me, and I thought I was oscillating and whirling in my chair. I clutched at it—weak, miserable, and swamped in unsurpassable physical and mental suffering. I sensed that I was about to lose consciousness. I was going to fall helplessly to the mosaics on the floor, and I probably moaned in pain. Every so often that brutal hand held me up by the hair and shook me barbarously, while the voice continued to explain my case with an enthusiasm more fitting to some worthier object.

The nurse, who was standing by my side holding me by the arms, watched all the while. She finally tried to interrupt him and said, "The poor man is wracked with pain! He's going to faint!"

But the head man, bent on showing off my agitated nystagmus to his visiting colleague, did not listen to her and kept right on. Sensing that I had her support, I turned toward her as best I could and pleaded: "Ether! Give me ether!"

Where did that idea come from? Instantly she was off, returning with a jar and some cotton soaked in that volatile stuff. I inhaled it with a vengeance. I felt revived. I can still remember the look of censure, almost of hatred, that she cast at that unfeeling, indifferent hangman.

What makes women so good, so sensitive to our pain? Is it, perhaps, a kind of generalized motherliness? Or is it perhaps that because they suffer more they have a better feel for the pain of others? There is so much we owe women and so much we expect from them. There is so much we have to repent for, and so much we need to understand and make up for.

I left the clinic without the man's having said a word to me or shown me an attentive gesture, without his having given me any indication that he saw in me a human being. But the memory of that nameless nurse (tall and beautiful to me, like a statue), full of solicitude for a stranger (a mere house case), would join that of Miss Goldis to give me a new vision of Woman—impersonal and fraternal—and a new respect, tolerance, and sympathy for her problems.

Tenderly and compassionately, the nurse tucked the blanket around me, wheeled me out of that den of humiliation and inflicted pain, helped me compose my tortured head, murmured I know not what consoling words, and returned me to Dr. Bigby and my refuge.

This first return to the world of the living, after I had overcome the ultimate barrier, only made me desire more intensely the rapid resolution to my case—by annihilation.

On reentering my bed and my rest, and notwithstanding that I was crushed and exhausted, I had only one thought: "Why don't they just let us die in peace? Why are they prolonging this?" Dying seemed to me, then, to mean freedom and forgetfulness. It was not death that terrorized me. It was this inglorious and degrading suffering that came from being handled like a thing, a nothing, a nobody—this total loss of personality when one was turned into a "case"—which was much more painful than the piercing stabs that continued to split my head. Along with that suffering, there came to the fore as well the idea of slow decomposition that was already operative in my life.

(Now do not suppose that this picture of hardened professionalism and personal cruelty applies universally. On the contrary, it is those features of devotion, humanity, and sacrifice, so frequent in medicine, that I wish better to emphasize by contrast. One swallow does not a summer make.)

After this experience I felt too debilitated and depressed to attend even to what was going on around me. I know that the head nurse who had treated me so badly returned to tell me harshly that I was not a "bed patient," and that since I was not bedridden, I must take my meals in the refectory, along with everyone else who was ambulatory. Remaining where I was, with eyes closed, I replied: "I don't want any lunch, thank you."

The morning passed with intolerable slowness. Moans, cries, and the sounds of labored breathing broke up the uneasy, disturbed, tired, and somnolent peace of the ward. It was like being on another planet. Again I began to feel, with indescribable comfort, that this place was my place. I had crossed the barrier and now belonged to this world, the world of men who were "finished," men who were now at death's antechamber. I no longer held membership in the club of the living. To me what remained of life was an evanescent illusion. I was in limbo. And now, from the depths of physical misery and while consciousness had not yet forsaken me, I had to rise up to face the fact of my own disintegration.

It was necessary to confront death—if only with half a face and half a smile. Thus, feeling calmer, I lay there, motionless, in wait. It would not be long before I received my visit.

On the other side of the gangway, my pale interlocutor lay there, his eyes closed, as if having communicated his message, he now had nothing else to tell me.

III

I had plenty of time to reflect. This thing—facing death—what is it?

Many people die in combat, in accidents, and, alone and frightened, at the hands of an assailant, a sadist, a lunatic, without having even the time to commit their souls to God or the Devil. In a trench or at the barricades, a man in perfect health will nevertheless know that he might "cash in his chips" suddenly or that he might agonize in mud for hours and days, bleeding, helpless, cut to pieces by the pain, before turning totally cold in the blessedness of unconsciousness and insensibility. He also knows that there is the chance that he will escape with his life.

But in this place?

Here it is different. In the wards (especially the neurological ward) of a large public hospital in New York, which is itself a kind of drain for the emergencies of a conglomeration of nine or ten million human beings, death goes around constantly, slowly, fulminating. The expected thing, it is current, quotidian, *á la minute*. It has to be faced, coldly and serenely. There is time to see, think, and decide. Time to fear and time to fabricate courage. Physical pain is of little importance. Here either there is courage and acceptance or a sovereign fear dominates everything. But the rule is be quiet, obedient, and respectful—if not, they will tie you to your bed. The thing to do is die, but do it slowly.

My father used to formulate the wish differently—"to die, quickly"—but he himself lay in agony for long days and nights. He had, however, lost consciousness, regaining it only for brief periods shortly before he expired. As for me, here I am enmeshed in the throbbing coils of a serpent of pain that progressively twists itself through me. Inside me, there is something alive, insidious, creeping, draining me, slowly drilling its path through neurons and nerves, tissues, and vessels, destroying, corroding, decomposing, dissolving the best of my substance, proliferating at my expense—not just a threat, not solely a question of luck or chance, of holding bad or good cards, but something inexorable, perhaps ineluctable, which makes itself ready to carry me off through jungles of agony and pain to the purely mineral world.

It was to this, and only this, that I had to submit, to resign myself to, to become an impotent and passive spectator of my own dissolution.

Or else . . .

I was about to learn what else. It was to rear up, rebel, and fight, using the weapons of science, resistance, and will—and those of human cooperation.

I looked toward the door.

Suddenly there was silence, and Dr. Foster Kennedy appeared.

He was accompanied by the members of his general staff, among whom was my dedicated friend Nilson de Rezende. An aura of quasi-military discipline pervaded the ward. The patients were motionless, and the (impeccable) nurses were lined up, waiting. After a brief low-voiced exchange of impressions, the group advanced toward my bed, and their examination commenced. Pulling myself up with great difficulty, I exposed my misery.

The nystagmus, the inert side of the face, the wild gaze, the weakened arm and enfeebled hand, the leg slack and incapable of holding me up; the staggering and sinuous gait, unstable equilibrium, an inability to put my index finger to my nose—this all showed forth within the attentive and grave sight of those men and under the Master's brief instructions.

Afterward they poked at me, scratched me, touched my whole body from head to foot. They examined my sclerotic sensitivity, my pupillary reactions, the back of the retina; they carefully scrutinized my nose, my ears, and my mouth; they tested my senses of smell and taste. I vaguely identified some of the scents, but salt, sugar, and quinine bitterness were to me three undifferentiated white substances. High up in my head, from one side of the skull to the other, rang a diapason. Light burned into my brain, the slightest sound knifed through me, eczema spread out from its source at the left ear, dystrophy manifested itself inside the cheeks, internal compression at the back of the nose very nearly stopped my breathing, and my arms got heavier and heavier.

The examination and the questioning was carried on in an almost religious silence, with an occasional brief comment murmured through clenched teeth so that the patient could not make it out. To all this I submitted with the goodwill and curiosity of a guinea pig, one who could at least cooperate in research done by doctors who showed themselves to be solicitous, attentive to my suffering and committed to attenuating that suffering, almost pitying, and in any case very tactful. This was very different from the ear clinic. There was not a word or a gesture that might convey an observation or conclusion capable of upsetting and alarming the patient.

The group moved off, and for a few minutes Dr. Kennedy lectured his attentive and respectful retinue in inaudible whispers. The silence continued, broken only by moans and sighs.

For whatever reason, perhaps in the spirit of orderliness, I tried in my fumbling way to pull the night table closer to the bed. It had been pushed aside for the examination. Its metal legs scraped the floor, producing a tearing screech that shattered in two the august silence and froze me with pain and constraint.

Foster Kennedy come over to me, a warm smile showing on his clean-shaven face, and said, "Just lie still. Don't worry. We are here to care for you. We are going to administer penicillin—millions of units. Good-bye."

He gripped my hand vigorously, as if I were suffering merely from a wart on the nose, and rounds continued with another patient.

Once again the head nurse was at my side. She bristled, "Are you the fellow who made the table screech? Don't try that trick again. Dr. Foster Kennedy wants absolute silence when he is here."

There was no point in trying to explain. The Master's silence on the matter had already forgiven me my offense. I felt suddenly that I had delivered my life and my hopes into his hands. Nothing else mattered. (Curiously, I would never again see that harsh creature, who along with that anonymous butcher in the ear clinic, constituted my only inhumane souvenirs of that illness.)

When, after a while, Rezende reappeared, I asked him, "Well, what does the Master say? Will they operate? Yes? No?"

"For the time being, no. But if an abscess forms, then an operation is possible. For now they are going to fill you up with penicillin and vitamins. You are in good hands."

"Thanks to you, old man. But tell me. What if there were no penicillin?"

"They would give you sulfa drugs."

"And if. . ."

"Oh well, old man, it's better not even to talk about that. But there's nothing to worry about. Nothing."

They brought me my lunch (I was a bed patient after all). I tried to eat while lying on my back, but I started to gag. My friend was alarmed. "You are going to choke."

Did he fear (discreetly) that paralysis of the glottis was impeding my ability to swallow?

Was it then, or later, that my wife returned from her conversation with the Master? It was around that time, in any event, that he told her: "We don't know what it is. We don't even know if we can save him. We promise nothing. Your husband is in danger. We count on a patient's stamina and the efficacy of antibiotics."

Suddenly I was alone. I prepared myself. My perspective was altered. Within, I set myself firmly on a non-material will, standing in the shifting sands of doubt. I forgot the outside world and concentrated on the battle that was just beginning. On my side I had Kennedy and penicillin, my sturdy spareness, a heart that was still sound. And amidst the barks coming from the moribund and the distressing cries of those who were scarcely alive, the sudden desire to engage in combat, to resist, and to vanquish radiated energy through my nervous system.

Late that night still another doctor, a stranger, appeared. He was accompanied by Dr. Galen, the sub-director of the infirmary. (Below Kennedy, Chief of Services, there was still Dr. Ross, the Director of the Men's Infirmary. From that moment on they paraded before me all the professors of neurology and their assistants from New York and Cornell Universities—specialists, researchers, and many other top people.) This chap examined my eyes and, turning to Galen, said, "The retina in the left eye is wasting away. Can he still see at all well? Poor man. Don't give him any injections during the night. Let him get some rest, at least."

Was he trying to say that I was in danger of going blind? That there was no remedy for it and that therefore it would be better not to torture me with treatment?

Dr. Galen smiled impassively, looked at me understandingly, and said, "Boss's orders."

The next day my friends began to stream in. In the afternoon (it was already getting dark out) there arrived a child, just over twenty. She was someone I had taken to considering as virtually my daughter. When she leaned toward me to get a closer look, I had a moment of weakness and turned my face to the left to hide my deformity.

"Don't look at me," I said, "I'm not the same person."

"To me you will always be the person you were."

Tears darkened her shining eyes. Yes, I found it difficult to face the living, with my half-a-face, my left eye staring wide-eyed, and my half-smile. I wanted to be left alone with my misery and my battle. If they would only go away and leave me in peace.

They moved me to the first bed on the other side, next to the windows, where I was able to enjoy a bit more quiet and privacy. From there, through the enormous windows dark with filth, through the screens and confusion of bars surrounding a kind of terrace, I could look out beyond the hospital's snow-covered walls to the cars that ran along the East River Drive, the vacant lots, the rusted buildings in the port, the wide river with its boats, ferries and tugs, and further on, the docks, the outlines, the fumes and fogs of Brooklyn, all of which made me nostalgic for the distant sights of the Lisbon of my childhood.

My departure for this new bed disappointed my neighbor from Harlem. After all, it now appeared that I would not be operated on. He felt, perhaps, that I was to blame for this rupture in our solidarity. He became sullen.

It is good to have friends, to feel that in difficult times we are not alone in the circular arena. And the nights underscore and accent one's feelings of gratitude at having them. Many of my

friends came, all of them offering to be of help. They would com-
mend me to the staff. Two of them, Maria and Francisco Keil
Amaral, who were off at some distance on a research trip to Michi-
gan, soon returned to New York, and they offered me the comfort
of their company and precious moral support. They did much to
keep our daughter, then aged five, entertained and distracted. They
got everything ready for Christmas and even kept the house while
my wife was rushing around to see doctors and visiting me in the
hospital. They took care of a thousand difficulties.

Other friends—Portuguese-Americans—helped me. They wrote
to the doctors telling them favorable and flattering things about
their patient. That undoubtedly created for me among infirmary
personnel an ambience more favorable than any surrounding an
anonymous patient. I felt privileged.

On the second or third day, Dr. Foster Kennedy decided to give
me a blood transfusion. "Sometimes it helps in cases like this," he
said. A half dozen friends promptly offered blood. As I have said, it
was wartime and everything was scarce. Danton Coelho, the dear
Brazilian friend who had already given me precious help during my
Beth Israel stay, and to whom I had in 1941 dedicated the first
edition of *Where Night Ends,* used to visit me every day, either
alone or accompanied by his wife. Stoutly he stuck out his arm for
Dr. Dewey. "Indian blood, doctor—the Charruas. It's strong
blood. Do him good."

He was tall and thin, a gaucho from Rio Grande do Sul, and the
possessor of incomparable vitality and purpose. We had a great
friendship, despite our many different and discordant ideas. I
became deeply indebted, in my exile, to the Brazilians!

I do not know, nor did they tell me, whose blood was given to
me. Unfortunately, my system rejected the intrusion, and minutes
after the transfusion was started, I suffered a horrendous attack of
the shakes. It was worse than the attack I had incurred at Beth
Israel. Agitated from head to toe, I could not control the spasms in

my legs, my teeth chattered, and the bed-rails jangled in macabre orchestration. Dr. Dewey came running, and with an anxious expression, he (who was always impeccable and seemingly untouched) yanked out the apparatus and stood there watching me. It was then that I met the new head nurse.

She was an older woman, solid and stumpy, robust, and very gray. Mrs. Abbey was a native of Scotland. She spoke, acted, and gave orders like the quartermaster of a sailing ship. There was in her color and manner, in fact, much that was maritime, naval. When I was hit with the chills the whole ward was sent into turmoil. Mrs. Abbey, heading a brigade of helpers clutching emergency resources, came to my aid.

Lost under a mountain of blankets and buried among scalding hot-water bottles, I managed little by little to overcome the attack. Something was said about the danger of blood clots. I understood nothing of the matter.

Mrs. Abbey did not leave me for an instant. Leaning over me, she smiled at me, speaking to me as one speaks to a baby in a crib. She massaged me, tucked me in tightly, and uttered encouraging words. Solicitude, cordiality, and kindliness were still the gifts of this brusque and authoritarian woman who had spent more than forty years working at her hard-boiled profession. Her maternal voice, with its heavy Scottish burr, stirred my heart and spirit, even though my contracted jaws prevented my uttering a single word.

Days later I learned her story. She was born on a barge sailing an estuary in Scotland. Her father, an old sea dog, was the boat's captain.

"I spent my entire childhood on that barge, many a year hardly setting foot on land, looking out through cabin windows at the shore and the wharves. I was raised in the midst of creaking winches and squeaking pulleys, among curses and whistles and voices directing the maneuvering and unloading of cargo, in fogs and in the cold, rocked by the swells. I was already a little lady when

I managed to get my father to let me go to school. My dream was
to become a nurse—I was twenty when I came to America—and I
have never been anything else."

It was undoubtedly that early experience which had forever
instilled in her those brusque ways and even the gait peculiar to
seafaring people, as well as the occult kindliness of heart, that
esteem for human life, and her sympathy in times of crisis (still
another trace of the character of the authentic seafarer). A nurse of
the old school, she was not only practical and *sans-façons,* but capable of frightening energy and a quickness remarkable for one of her
age and weight, not to mention her arthritic condition.

I always enjoyed imagining what life must be like aboard those
barges (about which I knew from the rivers and canals of Flanders)
with their staterooms of varnished wood, lace-trimmed curtains in
the windows, an insularity of floating hearths, a feeling of errant
and solitary lives (something which always attracted me) like those
of the *forains* in their big wagons eternally on the move or stationed
in the squares of the villages painted by Vlamynck. All this served
to reinforce my affection for Mrs. Abbey.

I had not shaved before coming to the hospital, and for several
days afterward I was not able to get the barber to come. (I was
having my usual "bad luck with barbers.") My facial paralysis,
staring left eye, and beard of several day's growth (it was still almost
entirely dark) made me look sinister. Dr. Kennedy had already
joked, "If you still have that beard tomorrow, I shall refuse to see
you."

The barber was a placid, middle-aged Italian, well-informed
about death and disease. He was used to shaving cadavers. He had
about him something of the discreet gravity possessed by men of a
funereal pomposity and was always ready with words of condolence and the look of formal commiseration for the mourning
family. His hands were worthy of a king. But they left me with a
funereal sensation, and I no longer wanted to employ his compas-

sionate services. We were forbidden the personal use of cutting instruments, but after the barber's visit, for which I had waited several days, I was authorized to use a razor. I would shave myself while lying down, acrobatically holding the mirror above my head, with that wide-open and teary eye looking down on me. I detested my face.

But that was nothing. During the first few days I could see that I was getting worse. I continued to run a high fever, pain and muddle had increased, my vision had become more confused and was growing dark, and I felt very weak. Somnolence was taking possession of me. The interminable morning tasks on the ward and the disquieting nights full of cries and death rattles, with periodic interruptions for injections of penicillin and vitamins, the conversations and discussions of patients—everything troubled my rest. When I did manage to sleep, I slept with difficulty. I told the boss, in whose green eyes I saw reflected something or other. Was it that he feared a slow encephalitis? The lumbar puncture done when I arrived turned up nothing. They did not know what bacillus (or virus) was burrowing into my encephalon.

One afternoon, while dozing, I felt someone pulling at my leg and heard a voice calling, "Joe, hey Joe! Wake up!"

It was that "good old" doctor whose optimistic conviction that I was a hypochondriac had helped to put me where I was. I was annoyed.

"How do you feel?" he asked.

"What do you think!" I replied in bad temper.

Vexed with me, he turned to Dr. Galen, who was with him, and began to say, with a smile of abashed irony, that I had appeared at his office with a "list of symptoms," asking for treatment. Galen smiled imperturbably and looked at me.

From the bed I said, "Sure. For weeks I asked him to give me penicillin. And now here I am, in this hospital bed, taking penicillin."

Galen's smile broadened understandingly, and Dr. Z. disappeared beyond my horizons. (Months later I ran into him at some restaurant or other. He looked like he'd seen a ghost.)

Among the specialists that curiosity brought my way was the Englishman Dr. Atkinson. An older man, he was most courteous and charming, but impenetrable. Since diseases of balance and equilibrium were his preserve and domain, he examined me (at Dr. Kennedy's request) with minute attention, and when he was through he looked at me with an air of meditative gravity—one that indicated that he was intrigued and, perhaps, doubtful. He told me nothing.

Dr. Friedman from Berlin never ran into Professor Kennedy at the hospital. They were masters of the same trade. Both were big-time, and there wasn't room enough for the two of them at the side of the same patient. To me he always spoke in French—a rather mediocre French—as if we shared a kind of European solidarity, and he treated me as if I were, like him, a refugee. Short and stocky, with legs like pliers, he was what is called roly-poly, and he literally came rolling down through the ward yelling, "Where is my dear Portuguese friend?" Into that designation he would stick the adjective "liberal."

It was he who diagnosed the arachnoiditis (after the Master's initial diagnosis), and who one day, in investigating the results of the second lumbar puncture (Dr. Bigby's work), revealed the presence of some kind of leukocytes in the rachidian fluid. He frowned and said, "I don't like this at all." He feared, it seems, that the infection would spread to the bulb and would thus bring me to a fulminating death, similar to the deaths suffered by those individuals with bulbar poliomyelitis.

In a show of affection, Friedman stayed with me to the end of my illness. Weeks after leaving the hospital, I ran into him on Second Avenue. I was loaded down with heavy bundles. He eyed me. It was as though while somehow knowing me, he nevertheless did not recognize me. When I told him who I was, he was startled, surprised.

"What, sir, are you doing here?"

Had he expected to see me confined to a wheelchair? In a few years. . . . But let's leave that for later.

It was customary for instructors and students to congregate around patients, interminably repeating examinations and asking questions.

I never got to know, or have forgotten, the name of that Viennese master-teacher who would show up with his students in neurology. He was small, thin and wiry, with a waxed moustache and a heavy Germanic accent. One day he too asked me if I would allow myself (since, after all, I was the chief's patient and had no obligation to serve as a manikin) to be presented to his students.

I permitted it quite willingly, partly out of vanity at being a "rare case," and partly out of a desire to cooperate with medical science—the only compensatory service I could now render my fellow creatures. (Yes, even in our most abject misery we can take some consolation and pride—an idea that propped me up a good deal then. I thought of beggars who scrupulously cultivate their running sores.) It was not every day that a cerebellum case presented itself. The students got to the point of laughing around me, asking me for data, and I inspired them slyly as if it were all part of a classroom recitation.

"*Pontine angle*. But, for God's sake, do not shake the bed. It rattles my brains."

After going through the usual steps, which I knew by heart and could anticipate, the teacher sat on the bed. He then asked me to describe my symptoms and narrate the history of my case—anamnesis, I believe they called it.

I jumped at the chance and told my story with the relish and precision native to a hypochondriac. (I am convinced, moreover, that the majority of physicians are hypochondriacal, too, so strong is the vocation for this kind of study that this "mania" incites and cultivates. The crises of fear and nausea that medical students go through are fits of hypochondria—a personalizing of symptoms and syndromes. Horror at the cadaver is perhaps nothing but the fanciful impersonation of death. And it is possible that the love of diagnostics is merely an external manifestation of a personal disquietude. Think of how many physicians, terrified of their own symptoms, run to a trusted colleague to free them from their fright or try out for themselves the many medications and drugs they prescribe for us? Physicians are *persons*, and from that point of view, perhaps, they are much more tortured by anguish than are the ordinary run of mortals, their patients.)

At the end the Viennese doctor turned to his boys and excitedly commented, "Rarely can a patient give us such a clear, subjective description of his condition. Such a thing calls for powers of sharp observation and an uncommon ability at expression. Only a physician can do it—or a writer. *Ziz iz fery, fery imporrtant!* For example . . ."

And, in a striking evocation, he then told the story of a Viennese cardiologist who himself suffered from a case of incurable heart disease. At death's very door (and working by himself) he had inserted the probe of a registering device among his arteries and into one of the cavities in his heart. Seated before the device, watching the needle trace on a drum the graph of his drawn-out agony, he expired. They found him at his work table, face-down, pen in hand, his last word broken off.

"A hero and a martyr to Science!" the professor concluded eloquently, as he portentously shook my bed. The amused students smiled. Then the professor turned to me.

"What is your occupation?" (Your *racket*, he said in good slang.)

I told him what I did, how I earned my living, and that by vocation I was (woe be it to me) a frustrated, unfulfilled writer.

"Didn't I tell you?" countered the physician, flush with perspicacity.

Following this, he interrogated his students, and was delighted to find that they had made the right diagnosis, having been stealthily led to it by me.

The lesson ended on this note. "Cases like this are extremely rare, and hardly ever do they get to us *alive*. Frankly, this is the first one I have seen. Just a few days ago I performed an autopsy on an identical case—a great involvement in the cerebellum of the first, second, third par, and all the way down. *Total* devastation of the central nervous system!"

"I am much obliged for your encouraging prognosis!"

Around the bed everyone laughed. And I laughed along with them. They had turned me into a guinea pig. Theirs and mine. There I was, watching myself suffer as if I were somebody else. Despite the Master's (Kennedy's) extreme discretion, I had learned a great deal lying there on my sickbed. But now nothing could upset me. I was ready to win. I wanted to help them win this battle.

I had learned a great deal, and had had some fun, too.

IV

No, the ward did not have a happy ambience. A huge and very dark Negro was wheeled up to a bed, placed in it, and then tied down. He screamed convulsively. They had found him next to some railroad tracks, his head smashed in, but still alive and still operable. Obstinately, they were resolved to save him—if only to drag out his agony for several more days.

Up ahead in the ward, where I had been placed at the outset, the young woman surgeon continued to implore: "Mister Hartman, answer me! Mister Hartman, can you hear me?"

She did not want her patient to die. She wanted to take pride in having saved a life that stood already before the abyss. But Mr. Hartman responded only with a growl that each day grew weaker and more distant. He was sinking away, slipping from hands that were trying to retain him.

New patients were coming in all the time, some unconscious, some screaming and struggling. Few of them left the place— and then they were almost always wheeled out on a stretcher, covered with a sheet. The aides would come in and set up white screens around the patient's bed, and a solemn silence would descend on the place. Minutes later the screens were removed, and one more cadaver would roll out on its way to the morgue. Another one had "kicked the bucket"—to quote the picturesque popular expression. It would not be long before there was a rising din of conversation and discussion. But no one talked about death. That topic was taboo among all those candidates for the Grim Reaper.

On my left there lived (literally speaking) a young man about thirty, semi-paralyzed and in a wheelchair, who raised and lowered himself in and out of bed through a series of complicated movements and rituals, but with no help. He sweat it out alone, stubbornly. He had a Schubert-like head, was intelligent and quiet, read a great deal, spoke in a thick, husky voice, but seemed to be beyond (but not indifferent to) the dramas and miseries of the ward. He told me his story. At birth he had suffered a skull compression which had caused him permanent injury. To the age of eighteen he had been a pampered child, thriving in a mother's love. When she died there was no one else in the family who could take care of him. He became an asylum case. He went from institution to institution. It became necessary for him to make over his entire way of life. He had to adapt.

"I've been here five years," he told me. "But it won't be long before they complete the chronic-illness pavilion on Welfare

Island, and I will be going there for the rest of my life. It is a very good place and it's comfortable, with gardens, terraces, game-rooms, a swimming pool, everything."

He had sought out the most minute particulars of the hospice and spoke of it as if it were a palatial hotel. I marveled at his composure, given his adversity and solitude. So, I thought, it was possible to live like that, to accept one's fate without rebellion or bitterness, at least apparently. His situation was so much worse than mine. It is certain that, beyond money, he had other kinds of support. Whenever the rabbi showed up, the two of them spent a good deal of time conversing and praying in murmurs. Imprisoned for life, without having committed any crime other than that of being born, this boy read a great deal, was well informed, and showed a profound interest in society—in that living world that he hardly knew.

In front of me and to my left was Paul, the German. He had once been a cook. But now, suffering from advanced paralysis, he was immobile from the neck down. He was the center of attraction for the ambulatory patients. He talked, sang, and laughed, but for long stretches he became sad and fell into silence. He had once been a *ruban-bleu* in one of New York's great restaurants. But for many years he had been confined to the hospital because he did not want to be a burden to his only (married) daughter. "She has her husband and her children to take care of and the house, too. I won't be alive when I leave this place." He was the one who, from time to time, screamed out, "Nurse! Hurry!"—and someone would come running, but usually too late.

Then they would have to undress him, thoroughly wash him, and change his bedclothes—the whole transaction taking place amidst joking and laughter. How marvelous the nurse's patience, and his! Once in a while they would lift him out of bed and seat him near the windows, where some sun-rays peeked through. His head would droop, sleepily, and he would ask someone to lift his right hand and place it in such a way that it would support his chin. That was all the strength he had left.

December was slipping away (I celebrated my forty-fourth birthday in that place), and I would turn toward the immense windows, from which I was separated only by a night table and a battery of radiators, to look out at the rusted landscape. Thus far it had been a hard winter with much snow. The wind blew in, and mixing with the hot air from the radiators, which whistled day and night, caused the black-out window shades to slap and bang. The light sifting through the screens and dirty windows was sad. At times the sun shone brilliantly, far off. Both the sky and Brooklyn would take on the tints seen in old Dutch seascapes. New York maintains something indefinably Flemish—Dutch—in the contours of its ancient neighborhoods—Brooklyn and Greenwich Village—that will suddenly evoke for us the city's original name, "Nieuw Amsterdam." And I would think, "Why don't the painters paint this? Where are the painters, those who do not come here to paint?"

And I would wait, patiently, riddled with pain. At night the greenish-black shades were lowered, and at ten the lights were turned off. The only lights left shining were those at the end of the corridor, in the kitchen and in the pantry, from which there came to us the voices of the aides and the sounds of banging plates and metals. Just before this they would come by to offer us, from tables on wheels, milk, fruit juice, and, to the sleepless, sedatives.

Each night, like the day, is spent in lamentations and screams. Somebody is agonizing in the dark, the death rattles are intolerable. He won't let his neighbors sleep, and there are protests. A voice will yell out, "Shut up!" Or the voice will complain, "Bring out the stick!"—and the laughter spreads. A nurse comes to scold them. But the dying person finally shuts up, for good. They put up the screens around him, and there is, as usual, that instantaneous silence. Every day someone "kicks the bucket."

One particular night Dr. Kennedy appeared with an assistant. He came to look in on me and to ask some questions. It was 3 A.M. I opened my eyes and found him at my side, leaning toward me, looking me over, reflecting. Such solicitude moved me. He was dressed in white jacket and white tie, and about him there wafted the aromas of the party he had just attended. He was seventy-four, married to a rather young Spanish woman, and the father of a baby. Like a boy, he still danced away the nights, some indiscreet persons told me, and he drank as much as his intense social life required him to drink.

During one of his visits he stuck out his hand and ordered, "Squeeze this hand, please. Now with the left."

Suddenly he showed surprise. It was the only time he did so. My left hand didn't have nearly the strength of the right. He compared them. They were unequal in size, as they had always been.

"Do you play tennis?" he asked.

I said that I did. I lied, for I was ashamed both of the asymmetry of my hands and of the fact that, I must confess, I had never had the luxury to participate in sports. Then, letting me off the hook, he turned to his assistants and said, "When I was a boy, I played a lot of tennis. Because of that I could not slip my right hand, in contrast to the left, through the opening of a buttoned shirtsleeve."

Mentally I thanked him for that comforting observation. But I understood all too well its therapeutic significance.

Dr. Kennedy was a man of great vigor—red-faced, radiant, with a huge, very bald head and sculpted masculine features of a surprising regularity. Originally from Northern Ireland, I believe, he was already an adult when he came to the United States to practice medicine. He spoke in a murmur, through closed lips. Once, when he was listening to me through the stethoscope and grinding his teeth in a peculiar way, I noticed that he had a long scar running down his neck. Later I asked a mutual friend about that scar. They had cut into his carotid artery to remove a large blood clot which was rising to block and destroy his brain. From that time on I viewed him with redoubled admiration as a resurrected being.

"Imagine your luck!" he said to me, laughing. "Dr. Fleming has just written to me that for a week now he has been bedridden with a cold, and penicillin doesn't help him at all."

In my case, the penicillin was making visible progress. A week after entering Bellevue, my facial paralysis was beginning to recede. I was starting to feel some sensation as well as an itch on the left side of the upper lip. At least I was free of the abscess. But I continued to suffer, to feel distressed and debilitated. Retronasal compression seemed to be suffocating me, and there were no signs of suppuration. What was to become of that mass of pus that was pressing at the base of my skull? Nasal dripping gave me no relief. As an organ my nose was useless. I wanted some audacious surgeon to operate on me, to go through the roof of my mouth so that he could drain and scoop out the infected cavities, those sphenoidal recesses, perhaps, that I was then hearing so much about. I was forbidden to go to the bathroom or to take baths. The nurses bathed me in bed and rubbed me with alcohol.

The hospital day, as in a barracks, started at six. There was general cleaning, the bath, breakfast, a change of bedclothes, ventilation—tasks that dragged on because there was a dearth of personnel and too many patients.

But there were the young student nurses. Every morning the room filled up with those white swallows, youthful, fresh, animated. Ah, to me they were all pretty, and some of them really were beautiful. Was it their goodness and solicitude that made them so attractive? Those budding lives—rosy cheeks, white hands, red mouths—would look over and manipulate that collection of monsters, that veritable gallery of horrors that we were.

My half-a-face, stubble beard (as long as it lasted), my teary pop eye, my uncertain movements (whenever I stuck out my hand to grab some object, I knocked it over or missed my aim entirely), the summary wretchedness of my situation, none of this could I hide from my vain self or from their eyes, eyes in which I never came upon belittling pity or affronting repugnance. They made me feel like a different person—normal in a certain sense, natural, nearly perfect. They cared for us as if we were dolls or, possibly, babies. Once one of them took my hand, and surprised by it, said, "Such nice nails! Did you ask for the manicurist?"

Now I had always had the ugliest hands. They were gnarled and rough, besides being asymmetrical. Never in my life had I confided them, most certainly more out of timidity than as a matter of principle, to the care of a manicurist. My hands are the hands of my stone-worker and peasant ancestors. I recall the distant time when, under the influence of my melancholy reading, I imagined a story in which a man ended up having to live divorced from his own strange and frightening hands, and whose hands one night, under the spell of a morbid autonomy, strangled him. I never wrote the story because it was transparent to me that it was about a suicide, one carried out—let me put it this way—by "an intermediate person." I now notice that my story "The Stain Cannot be Effaced" turns on this same obsession with hands, and that the unfortunate character in "A Career Cut Short" has beautiful hands.

I smiled as well as I could and explained to the student nurse that I had myself cut and industriously filed my nails. Was it just that in that place she was used to seeing only rough, uncared-for hands? Or was she merely trying to flatter me—as part of her job, part of her technique to improve a patient's morale? And what if that were the case—so what? Such lies were good for us. They were sweet lies, like all those lies that offer us illusions. [But that patients fall in love with their young nurses is de rigueur.*]

---

*Recently an eminent American specialist recommended to student nurses that they make professional use of their "sex-appeal," which, according to him, is an adjuvant in the treatment of cancer in old men. The nurse is to be at one and the same time a species of secular working nun and seductive vamp—a really difficult combination. That the profession imposes onerous respon-

It was 8 A.M., and a pale gilded sun crept along the East River. One of the student nurses talked while she gave me bed-care. She asked me about my life, my likes and dislikes, what I did, my plans. No. It was not possible that the interest that I could read in the bright, dark eyes of this young Italian woman (she was called Miss Scarpa) was merely a professional trick. But even if it were? Every sick person loves to entrust, to believe. I talked about my business and the dreams I hoped to realize if I ever left that place alive—and with my head intact.

"What would you like to be doing at this very moment if you were back out there and healthy?"

I looked out at the East River, at that creeping sun (seen at second hand), at freedom and the world, through the bars and obstacles that separated me from all that, and suddenly I pictured myself under a clear, blue sky, dressed in shorts, running on a path between stretches of grass and along the calm waters of a canal, feeling the cool, sharp morning air on my bare skin, happy to be alive, free and in full flight, and feeling within me the energy and agility of my lost youth.

I told her about this very thing. Afterward I fell silent, overcome with emotion, and I turned toward her. Her beautiful eyes had followed my prisoner's gaze to the outside and had envisioned, perhaps, that clean and fresh scene that I had described for her. Her eyes had welled up in tears. Oh, the good Miss Scarpa!

Across the aisle, Paul, the paralytic, was talking excitedly with the youthful nurse my wife and I had taken to calling "Miss Park

---

sibilities on nurses helps to explain, certainly, why there is that dearth of nurses about which the New York hospitals complain. On the other hand, after the publication of the first edition of this small book, an illustrious Portuguese practitioner urged student nurses not to be carried away by the romantic element in the nursing profession. Treating the matter from the point of view of the hospitalized patient, I merely wanted to put into relief that aspect of nursing that is quasi-devotional.—*(Note to the second edition.)*

Avenue." We called her that because she was pretty, elegant, and had a distinctive way about her, though in comparison with her older colleagues, she did show a touch of pride and hardness. She talked to him, made him laugh, pulled away the covers from his inert, varicosed legs, lifted from the bed that invalid old cook's horrendous feet—livid, scaly, desiccated—and set about caring for them. She washed them with alcohol, clipped the nails, trimmed callous corns, and powdered the feet as one would powder a baby after its bath. Her perfect hands of snow and roses moved lightly, tenderly.

Throughout the entire procedure, which took some time, the two of them laughed. But I did not laugh. It was my turn to have tears in my eyes out of gratitude and tenderness for such humaneness and so much devotion. I shall never forget those feet, which reminded me of the feet belonging to Ribera's saints and monks. Nor will I forget those two hands, flitting about them, like the wings of a dove.

The "tough guy" of the ward—its black sheep—was a tall, thin Italian. A semi-paralytic, he dragged himself from bed to bed to complain about everything and everybody. Eternal lines of bitterness showed in his face, and his sunken eyes and earthen coloring gave him a spectral air. The nurses—he said—gave him no attention, and the doctors were to blame for his misfortune. One saw immediately in him that spoiled ex-momma's boy, the *latino,* the martinet, the constant complainer. He would lift up his faded hospital pajama tops, pull the bottoms down a bit, and show off an immense scar in the shape of a cross that ran from his ribs to the bottom of his chest, almost from one side to the other. He had been "operated on for ulcers." It must have been one of those exploratory operations, on the grand scale.

"Look. Look at what they did to me," he repeated over and over hollowly, going from bed to bed, like one who wants to discredit all doctors and hospital service—in this world and the next. "They did me in. They severed some nerve inside here, by mistake, and left me paralyzed."

For everything that goes wrong in this world the victim, the complainer, must find a scapegoat. The Italian played at cards, got involved in stammering disputes, and at night against all regulations, smoked beneath the covers, like a brat in an orphanage, endangering the lives of the thousands of patients in that immense complex. The smell of tobacco made me atrociously nauseous, but of course I said nothing.

The man suffered from hemorrhoids, and at any moment exposed them if anyone showed the least interest in the spectacle. From his bed he yelled continuously, "Nurse! This thing hurts!"

He insisted on care, special attention, medicine. And from time to time a nurse would come to treat his revolting ailment.

He came from a family of Italian immigrants, prosperous in appearance, probably Sicilians, typically living in lower Manhattan. One of his brothers had a rather ostentatious air about him. He was like a wild duck, a gangster exuding self-importance. His family visited him frequently, covering his bed with fruit, tidbits, and odds and ends, and filling the room with joviality, hullabaloo. The Italians are always charming, and not even in a desolate infirmary do they lose their keen sense of the picturesque and the spectacular.

It was this rebel, who in his impotence and dependence on public succor was always demanding the babying, the exaggerated attentions with which his mother had raised him so that he could bum around in the streets, that one day "Miss Park Avenue" had to put down and set straight. He had hidden a bottle of whiskey in his bed, and she found it. This was a grave infraction, above all in the neurological ward and by a patient of his stripe. The man floundered, but refused to surrender his bottle. She then showed us what a twenty-year-old is capable of when compelled to exchange her angel's role for that of law enforcer. She was like a master sergeant on inspection day. At the end of a war of words that put the ward in an uproar, the rebel, beaten and sullen, shut right up. He hid his head under the covers. The elegant young nurse's vocabulary measured right up there with that of any hooligan brought up on the streets of the Lower East Side. Her beautiful eyes flashed threateningly. In this journey through life one needs everything. There can be no doubt that this episode redoubled our respect for the swallows.

After the flock had departed, leaving the ward clean, scented, and provisioned, but also nostalgic, everything would fall more or less silent, and the patients would nap. There was as well a sense of fatigue in the air.

During the night, when called, different persons would appear, older women and helpers, many of them persons of color. (Manual tasks were then the province mainly of black women. Neither New York nor its hospitals had yet been invaded by Puerto Ricans of both sexes, who today hold so many of the low-level jobs in the hospital hierarchy.) There was one woman—white, seventy years old or possibly older, thin, garrulous, half-crazy—who on several occasions came to give me my periodic injections. She spilled out expressions of condolence and "tch-tch-tch-ing" each time she looked at my buttocks, riddled like a pin cushion. Then she would say, "You'll see. It won't hurt a bit. And it'll do you some good."

She would rub me vigorously with a wad of cotton soaked in alcohol, and then invariably stab the needle into the opposite side. There was one advantage in all this. Not expecting to get it there, I would allow that mass of muscles to remain perfectly relaxed, and the injection, with no resistance from me, would be administered without pain or risk of failure. It was always the other cheek I had contracted.

One night, kiddingly, I called it to her attention that she had made a mistake. There was a startled yell. "Is that possible? Tch-tch-tch! Excuse me." And off she went, having tucked me in maternally.

V

The Negro with the smashed head agonized for long drawn-out days and nights, in a grievous decrescendo.

Mr. Hartman fell permanently silent, as well. Days later I noticed that the aides were coming to set up the screens of white curtains around the bed of that pale young boy who had conversed silently with me on the morning I arrived. His death brought about a more prolonged and compassionate silence than was customary. Quiet, sad, always motionless, always expressing indescribable resignation as he suffered through consecutive operations, he had won over the ward's brutish heart.

Opposite my bed, on the other side of the room, there was a wide glass door that opened out to a covered terrace. It was dark, the color of brick and rust. Out there in the open air and in the winter cold were placed those beds that had been in recent use, beds in which, probably, someone had expired. Whenever a bed became empty it was dragged over to the terrace, and for each new patient—and they arrived with frequency—someone would go out there to get him a bed. That window-door remained open for the length of time it took to perform those maneuvers, and at such times there rushed into the overheated room a tremendous blast of freezing air, wrenching cries of protest from the patients. I would receive the full thrust of that burst of nordic hell, and would cover myself to the crown of the head, my teeth chattering, and curse to myself. But I just had to take it. All the prevention and precaution practiced by the doctors were of no avail when set against topography.

I had lost my senses of smell and taste, and much as my nose reacted to certain disagreeable stimulations, I hadn't the slightest notion of any odor that might come from bedclothes. Even so, when I looked at the washed sheets that they put on my bed, irremediably stained with blood, pus, and feces, I could not help feeling mentally nauseous. Lavender hospital pajamas, faded, dreary, and mismatched, would at times display blotches of a suspicious stiffness. My wife had at the outset brought me some inexpensive pajamas, which at least kept me from having to make direct contact with those sheets from which not even the pressure cooker could remove such evidence of illness, distress, and death. It was wartime, as Bigby had said.

One night I called for the bedpan. The old nurse answered my call, flustered and uttering her habitual expressions of encouragement. "Have no fear. This one is clean. I've just taken it out of the cabinet."

Given my debility, I was forced to use the pan lying down and in almost total darkness. At one point when the pan, dry and still warm from the sterilizer, touched my hands I felt something flake off—a kind of membrane. When, at last, the old woman returned with her flashlight, I saw, to my horror, that the old and dented nickel bedpan was completely covered with a coat of excrement. That was the "skin" which had flaked off and had left my sheet covered with repulsive scales and flakes. Some poor soul, perhaps already lying in the morgue, had left thereby the traces of his intestinal incontinence.

How was it possible, I think today, to endure all this without protesting, vomiting, jumping out a window? I controlled my horror as best I could, reminding myself that we live in a dangerous, germ-filled world, and that most of the time we manage to survive. That already having a generous dose of germs in my system, I could suffer little more from that contagion. And, finally, that doctors and nurses are in constant daily contact with these and worse horrors—and they live, laugh, eat, and make love. I did not feel that I had the right to complain like the Sicilian with the abdominal scar. And, besides, I took a certain pride in not behaving like a spoiled child.

Christmas was coming soon, and with its anticipation, came

the traditional preparations. There were streamers, ribbons, and curled paper flowers to decorate the ward, and a pine tree to set up next to the windows. A festive air prevailed. Some of the ambulatory patients helped the hospital personnel put up the decorations. At intervals Paul, the paralytic, sang in his deafening baritone voice the old song "O Tannenbaum"—which did not keep him from suddenly interrupting himself to call for the nurse, with the same result that we already know about. Someone would run to throw open a window so that the December wind could sweep from that dismal atmosphere the odor resulting from that meritorious struggle. And all those who could do so would laugh.

Outside, atop the hospital wall on the east side, they installed a Christmas tree several meters tall. Ornamented and illuminated, it now took its turn tinging the snow with multicolored reflections. With difficulty I could raise myself from my bed to get a glimpse of the tree in the clear, nighttime quietness. A strange placidity would possess me.

The young nurses, in white dresses, caps, and shoes, and navy blue capes, held hands and stood before the tree, in a circle, singing Christmas carols. Those fresh young voices brought to us from the outside, from the sooty city, the appeal of life and a lightly melancholy joy, which was like the promised rebirth that is always associated with this solstitial feast. And though the experience was sentimental, perhaps even banal, I found it consoling, sedating.

When they entered singing the most popular of the songs, "Adeste Fideles," this lonely Portuguese expatriate could not suppress his emotion. The whole infirmary fell silent, to listen to those voices, interrupted only by a dying man's growl or some recent arrival's painful cries.

It was 1945, the year of Hiroshima, the death of Roosevelt, the end of the war, and of a thousand enthusiasms and frustrated hopes, difficulties, and dark presentiments—and I was worried over the book that years earlier I had sent off to Brazil by diplomatic pouch, confiding it to the care of a friend who had generously assumed the task of getting it published. I had given it a title symbolizing my intentions—*Where Night Ends*. But lying in that hospital bed, I sometimes pondered the notion that my "night" was not coming to an end (as I had thought) but was only now beginning. And I wondered whether, even if I did leave that place alive, I would have the energy, mind, and imagination to give body and reality to that obstinate dream that had so long sustained me.

I had heard nothing regarding the book for some four years. The Allied censors, who held up all papers (I would later, after years of delay, receive letters accompanied by the British censor's "apologies"), had perhaps "archived" the proofs that a telegram from Rio de Janeiro in 1943 had promised me. Knowing how anxious I was and wanting to give me a boost, my wife one day secretly telephoned Rio and came back with news that could not help but bring me jubilation. "Dr. Jaime Cortesão wants me to tell you not to die. Your book is ready, the cover is in press."

That was always the tone of our conversations. I kissed her with great feeling and tenderness, and with much gratitude to my distant and brotherly friend!

But when she left I turned toward the windows, and for a second time I was overcome with emotion. I had not lived my life entirely in vain. At least I would leave the world a modest message, in earnest, at least, of the man I had wanted to be. And I thought with fear of what my existence would be like if having escaped death, I were then mentally inept, sterile, and impotent. Already I did not see well enough to read a book or a newspaper.

In the midst of such random dark thoughts—during my only instant of despair since those agonizing first few hours—I noticed that someone was standing by my bed. I looked up and saw Dr. Galen.

"What do we have here?" he asked. "Bad news?"

Stammering, sniffling, and drying my eyes, I told him what was going on, about the doubts that had suddenly embittered me. He put his hand on my shoulder, firmly but gently. "Don't worry. Only yesterday Dr. Kennedy assured us that you are out of danger and that you will once again be your old self."

His words carried so much peace, conviction, and simplicity that I could not help believing him. There are still good people in this world, I thought gratefully, and smiled. When one is in such spirits, even dying might be easy.

(My book appeared months later, and on a June day in 1946, another friend came running down through sand and pines to the beach he had offered hospitably to this convalescing patient for his recovery, waving over his head the first copy just in from Brazil. My "night" was over, and now, perhaps, my day was beginning anew.)

One afternoon a former patient returned to see Paul. He was an enormous and boisterous Russian, who had spent many months in the ward, stretched out with a weight attached to his head, to get back into place some tendons and a fractured bone—the results of an injury suffered one night when, imprudently twisting himself, he fell from a chair.

On the other side of the Atlantic these two men would have faced off as implacable enemies, but in the hospital they had become close friends. The Russian arrived loaded up with gifts for his "brother-in-arms." He went through the ward greeting his contemporaries, hugging the nurses, his booming voice filling the place. Paul introduced him to the newcomers to the house. To one another they talked excitedly, recalling their camaraderie of yesteryear, and when the visitor got up to leave amid grand gestures and thundering cries, Paul was left truly alone. This spirited, jovial man, who was the living example of good humor in the midst of misfortune, broke into a child's lamentable crying. It was difficult to console him.

"He is my brother, my brother! I have no other," he screamed.

"And I shall never see him again. I won't be around, next Christmas."

One morning, following the usual commotion, there arrived by stretcher a man of thirty-some years. He was stout and muscular, an authentic type in the New York, Paris, and Lisbon street markets. He was followed by his wife, whom I could easily have taken for one of those Portuguese fishwives who put on airs of prosperity. He went straight to bed, in front of me, at the corner opposite the windows. He howled in pain, arguing with himself like a madman, his eyes turbid and frantic. He screamed, "Water! Give me water! Molly, a drink! Gi'me a drink! Where are you?" He spit out, in every direction—a thick green substance. "Help! Help! My head is killing me!"

Exasperated and blind, he tossed and turned, rolling his head on the pillow. He would turn to the concerned people around him who were trying to keep him in bed. Mrs. Abbey tried vainly to calm him down. He howled and struggled. "This head is killing me! Molly! Molly! Give me a glass of water!"

Dr. Bigby rushed to do a spinal tap, and fluid, under tremendous internal pressure, spurted out and spouted to a great height, barely giving the physician a chance to avert his face. The patient's problem, in the cerebrospinal area, was in an irremediable phase. Why had those people waited so long? Molly, her arms crossed, stood serenely next to the bed, looking at her husband. What were her expectations in the matter?

"Nurse! Nurse! Call the doctor! Hurry! My head is killing me!"

Before long they transferred him, still spitting, over to a bed near the entrance. His cries reached me from a distance, becoming increasingly hoarse but growing more and more muffled, until I could no longer hear them. It was not long before they surrounded him with screens. There was the customary fall of silence, and shortly thereafter they took him out just as they had brought him in, wheeling him out on a stretcher, though now he was immobile, quiet. Following him still was his Molly. Some of the patients heaved sighs of relief. His turbulent presence had bothered them. Even that place required some tranquility.

When my wife returned that afternoon, she told me that she had seen Molly, an oilcloth bag hanging from her arm, quietly window-shopping on First Avenue. Molly was calmly going about as if nothing had happened to her, as if her only task was to price cretonne bedroom curtains she had for some time been thinking of buying.

"The dead go quickly!" I commented, disagreeably. And there came vaguely to mind Zola's story, the one entitled, I believe, "How One Dies."

These *fait-divers* of the infirmary (that terminus and drain for so much human misery, that solution to so many conflicts and incidents which to the normal living being pass unnoticed)—the almost daily elbowing with death and, worse, the need to deal with the final degrading aspects of human refuse—what influence, beneficial or degrading, could they have on the spirit of a patient whose mental integrity and life are threatened? Well—*none*.

Each one of us—as Death's guest—was, I suppose, committed to his own battle, to a decision already made, either to conduct the simple and elementary business of living, like the semi-paralytic to my left, or to prepare for that inevitably brief crossover, like the cook Paul—each was committed, in sum, to a species of egoism.

The only one who did not seem to be following "the rules of the game" was the man with the abdominal cross-shaped scar. He continued to stick to the laws of normal life and to the momma whose petting had spoiled him and of whom he spoke constantly. He railed against his irrevocable orphanhood, his hopeless situation, the doctors, the food, the nursing care, all that constituted responsibility and illness and represented the prospect of death. His egoism was still the egoism of the living or those who stubbornly insist on appearing to be among the living. That egoism was different from ours. Ours was the egoism of those who have delivered themselves over to the sole task of dying, of dialoguing with Death.

No longer, therefore, did anything so affect us as to alter the position of any one of us before his own personal problem. To become familiar with Death is to take away all its "romance," and suffering itself, when one is up against it, becomes a personal question each one resolves for himself in a tête à tête which may appear tragic to anyone looking on from the outside, but which is, for the patient, an absorbing and decisive game.

The solitude each man has within himself, this combat and this destiny, this self-absorption and estrangement from the world, this (dare I write it?) egoism is one of the most astounding and, at the same time, most consolatory things that illness offers us. All connections with the world are severed, and all those factors in life that have nothing to do with physical survival are scorned. Even as we come into life, alone and with obstinately personal effort, so, too, do we battle—whether to sustain that life or to face the end.

For some, that isolation is overseen by a God. For others, there exists only the darkness of nothing. But for many, certainly—the lost—there exists nothing more than indifference, passivity, hope, and in the end—possibly—peace.

A physician (and poet) once told me that on one occasion, at the urgings of the family, he had successfully revived (through injection) a patient who had just expired while under his care. When he opened his eyes, the recipient of this miracle had said merely, "Just let me rest!" I myself witnessed the prolonged agony of a woman at whom at every moment were directed her family's screams. They screamed out her name in the absurd, egoistic hope that they were consoling her, keeping her alive, and conveying the feeling that she was not alone. The poor woman made an incredible but vain effort to reopen sunken, dimmed, lost eyes that were already turned to eternal landscapes.

Bellevue Hospital, an immense pile of red and pink brick, has a nonsectarian chapel—Catholic, Protestant, and Jewish. To that chapel, indifferently, pell-mell, come the world's races. That this is the case has nothing to do with the then common call for "a racial melting pot." To live together in harmony does not mean to fuse. The rabbi conversed with my neighbor to the left, and they prayed together, in a whisper. The Protestant minister appeared at the door, off at a great distance, and cast irritated looks at that Gehenna wherein agonized an indescribable rabble. Perhaps he saw no one there conscious enough to be capable of raising himself to the direct and personal contemplation of God. The restive, timid Catholic curate continued to try out his question, "Is there anyone in need of my services?" I never saw anyone ask for him. It even got to the point that he was whistled and jeered at. He would leave angrily. (It should be noted, moreover, that the great majority of New York's population is made up of Catholics: Italians, Irish, Poles, Hungarians, Hispanics of various origin, and so forth.)

I do not know how many times I was X-rayed—a good half dozen, I'd say. The boss wanted to study the pictures of my case. Almost always it was Dr. Dewey who would take me to the radiologist's. All down the corridor there were patients lined up, on stretchers and benches, in wheelchairs. Once I was on the mirror-like table of the X-ray machine, making every effort to maintain myself in the most fantastic position—a sort of acrobatic "ponte," supporting myself on elbows and feet, my head turned back and down, and the apparatus pointed at my gullet so as to reveal the secrets of my sphenoidal cavities—when another patient showed up. She was a pale young woman, with the most regular features, and who, eyes closed, lay motionless beneath the sheets. She let escape a sharp, prolonged, frightened moan—one which could have served as the recorded sound for a ghost movie set in the castles of Scotland. It was lugubrious, feral, a canine howling, a cry from the forest primeval of a profound and forgotten animality, one that was particularly chilling for having come out of the closed mouth of an impassive, expressionless face that revealed not one sign of emotion or suffering. It was a cry of pain without pain, like a lament from another sphere, one of suffering antedating all reason and consciousness. Never again did I hear or do I ever hope to hear from a human throat anything like that voice.

Dr. Dewey said with some alarm, "Excuse me, this case is of great urgency."

I rolled off the table as quickly as my torpid motions permitted and onto the stretcher. I was distressed but pleased to know that there was a case more urgent and certainly much more harrowing than mine.

Not again would I be X-rayed. No matter. After all, what importance can there be in knowing whether or not my illness radiated from the sphenoidal recesses, now that the years have passed and all that remain are memories and a few dents?

VI

I had entered the place on the 29th of November, the anniversary of that distant day in 1918 when in a room in the Hospital de São José in Lisbon my twenty-three-year-old brother had died in my arms. I was only sixteen. This coincidence was not one to inspire confidence in anyone suffering from superstitious tendencies, which was not my case, though Bellevue, gigantic and incomparably more modern, along with having its own deficiencies, is the New York equivalent of our old institution. Still, like a university or a factory, a hospital is not a building—it is a function, a service; it is whatever, in sum, *men* make of it.

Would I end up like my brother? Of my past life, what hurt me the most was the idea of leaving behind my eighty-seven-year-old mother without having embraced her and consoled her a little for my prolonged absence.

When the thought of death came over me, I tried vigorously to find ways to repel the thought or to accept it as natural. I took consolation from the other cases in the ward—the incurable ones (like Paul), the pale boy who had died of a tumor of the nervous system, or the semi-paralytic to my side. And there were so many others! There was the chap with amnesia who read the newspaper end to end twenty times a day without ever knowing what was going on, and who promised to introduce us to his son, a Pacific war hero, the next time he came to see him—when the son had just that moment left his presence and had been introduced to all of us. And there was the good old Galician, the advanced paralytic—always sweet and in good humor—who nurtured hopes of improving, as well as the Pole who wept and blessed the name of Foster Kennedy: "I owe him my life. He is a second father to me."

The Pole would tell us how for months he went from doctor to doctor, made the rounds of clinics and hospitals, and no one had hit on the cause of his malady. He could not move his legs or, later, his arms. He collapsed into a wheelchair. He was a worker, an experienced mechanic. Then one day somebody was inspired to send him to the Master, who examined him and then, placing a finger on his cervical vertebrae, said, "Your sickness is right here. A tumor that presses on the nerves. You're lucky. It's not in the medulla. We shall operate and in a few weeks you will be well."

The man stared at me out of tear-filled eyes. "Already I can feel a tingling sensation in my legs, and I can move my arms. I can feel life seeping back into my body. May God bless him! I owe him my life."

Dr. Ross appeared, surrounded by some visiting people, and asked me if I minded being examined. Not at all. For the first time the interrogation took on the aspects of psychological probing. It was evident that Dr. Ross had *ideas,* and did not want to confine himself to the merely somatic signs of the malady. I myself had noticed that my speech was slower, and that from time to time I reversed syllables. For example, instead of "giddiness" I would say "digginess," a nonexistent word which is comic, moreover, for it seems to suggest "digging."

Imagine what being aware of this anomaly would mean to someone who had always spoken fluently, who had always taken scrupulous (if spontaneous) care with his pronunciation and diction. Even worse than this was my inability to read books or newspapers. They were all trembling gray masses from which, in my ocular spasms, I could pick out only the large letters. The slightest of visual efforts brought me immense discomfort. Perhaps the retina had been affected. I was in danger of losing the ability to perform what was most cherished and essential to me. Did I think about that? Perhaps I did not want to believe it. Or was I still hopeful? Maybe I had resigned myself to my fate. Or was I merely unaware of the truth? I do not know. What sort of existence could I expect, if I were to be so limited—permanently?

Dr. Ross pointed to common things—a cuff link, a tie bar—and asked me to name them. When I discovered that he was checking to see whether I was suffering from perturbations in speech or from memory and recognition failure, and trying to assess the extent of such changes, I became uneasy. What all this proved, as I saw it, was that the infection (or was it a lesion?) had disseminated far beyond the focal point of its beginning and was now threatening the greater centers. If it were demonstrated that I was suffering from lacunae in recognition and memory, though still only verbally, and from regressive loss in those areas, I would have to feel that my mental and intellectual integrity was even more threatened. I would be facing a much more difficult readaptation to habitual life.

For the first time I alleged that the interrogation was becoming distressful, especially given my limited knowledge of psychology and physiology. Curiously, one of the doctors present supported me against Dr. Ross. He agreed that the whole thing might very well aggravate a patient's anxiety. The elegant and a bit magisterial Dr. Ross turned white, smiled, and concluded: "All right. We did not come here to torture you." And he went away.

I became heavyhearted. When all was said and done, there I was in a public infirmary. Like the Sicilian, I was a house patient, and to them—doctors and men of science—a human guinea pig at everyone's beck and call. Dr. Ross's interest was legitimate, even praiseworthy.

They came to ask me, on the Master's behalf, if I objected to being presented at neurology rounds in the hospital's amphitheater.

"I'll go wherever he thinks it necessary."

It was after 11 P.M. when they came for me. I rolled clumsily from the bed onto the stretcher, and after many turns we entered the dark and naked antechamber of the amphitheater. Foster Kennedy came to meet me. He was cheerful and cordial, and said to me: "Please excuse this inconvenience, but your case interests us greatly, and I want my colleagues to see it. Since you are now out of danger, there is no problem whatsoever. I am most pleased with you. See you soon."

Pleased with me! It was just like Dr. Isaacs. But isn't it natural that a clinician who feels good about his work will take pride in the patient who rewards his efforts?

He returned to the amphitheater, and then I heard the voice of Dr. Bigby expounding my antecedent history with some inexactitude in the details. Then the Master spoke in an undertone, but I was unable to make out what he said. At last I entered the scene, wheeled in on the stretcher, and Foster Kennedy, smiling, interrogated me, and examined me briefly. There were, perhaps, about a hundred physicians seated on benches, listening attentively to the lesson. To all of them I was merely "the *pontine angle* head infection." The Master added the finishing touch: "How do you feel now?"

"Much better. But I still have pain."

He smiled. "Your headaches now are merely a writer's headaches."

He shook my hand. The session was over, and I was returned to the darkened ward, to the moans and anguished cries of the neurological night. My head really did hurt, and it would continue to hurt for a long time to come.

On the day before Christmas the Master appeared before me, accompanied only by the impassive Dr. Galen. He did not come in his white gown. The room was unusually quiet. Outside the sun was shining. He sat on the radiator case next to the windows, crossed his legs, and smiled at me.

"Today we are going to stop all treatment. I have decided to send you home this afternoon—warmly wrapped—so you can spend Christmas with your family."

He paused, then added, "You know, Sir, you are very lucky. You are the first patient of your kind that I have seen *alive* and conscious. You should be proud of that. I am. Don't ever forget that we owe it all to the great Fleming! Without him . . ."

He completed the phrase with an evasive gesture, and turned to Galen: "I have been a neurologist for forty years, and—since his arrival—I have wracked my brains, searched my books, and ransacked my files without finding another case like his. By the time they got to us they were all dead men."

I was moved, and wanted to sit up in bed, but I lost my balance.

"Careful," he said. "You're not about to complicate things by falling out of bed, are you?"

I told him then about my concerns. Wouldn't my illness leave me intellectually impaired? Would I be able to work at my former activities?

"You will be your old self," he replied. Then, after a moment of serious reflection, he added, "Ninety percent of that self."

Mentally I discounted further: "Seventy-five percent, if that." My "facial" had nearly disappeared and the other symptoms were diminishing. I no longer had that piercing pain. But there was, persistently, a residue of nystagmus. I was still seeing double, and my gait remained uncertain.

"You will go home this very afternoon. Rest. I want to see you back here during my office-visit days."

He left. I was overwhelmed with emotion. We began our preparations for leaving. I said my farewells to my companions in the ward. Paul was teary-eyed. The poor fellow would so habituate himself to his "companions" that he found it hard to see them go off, leaving him behind to await his final resolution. One of my Portuguese friends came to get me in his car. I was not able to say goodbye to the young nurses, for they had already flown off to other skies of pain.

When I set foot on the snow in the streets, supported on both sides and still stumbling, I had a feeling of recoil. The forms and colors, the bustle, it all seemed strange, monstrous. The world was unrecognizable, in every way deformed, as if seen through panes of dirty, irregular glass. To walk on the rough, hard snow crust was an ordeal. I would sway, lose my balance. My eyes did not focus as they should. I lost sight of things. Passing automobiles seemed to be moving along on discontinuous balconies. The familiar ambience had lost its habitual perspectives. Was that the world to which I must return? I felt the desire to rush back to my place, my shelter in the infirmary, where nothing was demanded of me but passivity, the inertia of acceptance.

Our friends the Keil Amarals had decorated the house, which was warm and inviting. I resumed my normal routine. The next day or so I sat down to write a postcard. I felt my way along, but the effort caused me to pass out. When again would I be able to read? How long would it take me to complete my slow return to that seventy-five percent that I counted on? Would I be the same person—though diminished? I had to confront my limits, pull myself out of that semi-darkness, reeducate myself, once again accept the everyday struggle, push myself ahead (though dazed and hobbled), and live (as Dubreuilh of the *Mandarins* would say) as if death did not exist. I must live my life among those men who struggle, who suffer.

From time to time I felt anew the impulse to retreat to the hospital. I was frightened, in pain. Whenever I tried to carry on a conversation, my fever returned. Humidity bothered me, the irritation in my nose had got decidedly worse, and I had bouts of bronchitis one after the other. I spent most of my time lying down or sitting with my left leg out straight and motionless, listening to the radio—to music or to the international debates at the incipient U.N. I had developed some cervical arthritis, and after meals my nystagmus got bad.

When I went to Kennedy and told him all this, he commented, "Well, I wouldn't advise your giving up eating because of that." He wrinkled his brow. "Who told you you had nystagmus?"

"Everybody was talking about it in my presence." And I told him about the incident at the hearing clinic. The Master shook his head. But who would now take the trouble to search out those who had been indiscreet (there had been so many of them)? And I did feel so very grateful to all of them. It was useful to know that, and other things, too. (In general, the American doctor does not treat his patients with frankness. He does not sort things out for the anxiety-ridden hypochondriac's benefit.) Besides, I had read books. I had read up on physiology.

Now, like thousands, like millions of others before me, I had to get used to living with the consequences, the small quotidian hardships, the limitations peculiar to my state. Therein lay the difficulty, and if there were such a thing, the "heroism"—not in a resigned passivity before death. But is it indispensable, or even possible, to live always in optimum health and the best disposition?

Perfect health does not exist, or if it does exist, one can never achieve it, for life is always in indeterminate decline. Constant complaining is the refuge of the impotent, the indolent, and the cowardly, who so manage things that they do not have to shoulder any responsibilities. They live off those persons next to them, their charity and their sacrifice—like the man with the cross-shaped scar. There is always somebody worse off than you are who nevertheless continues to live his life. I would look at the hundred-year-old trees in Stuyvesant Park, covered with lichens and fungi, eaten by worms and parasites, split open by lightening, lashed by wind and snow. They were alive. They endured, they flourished. Each year they covered themselves with new leaves. They gave us shade and respite from the heat. Nor should we, for that matter, wait to experience our "moment of creative power" before "making" and "producing." The moment is this one, right now, as Stendhal said. Genius and creativity are the products of effort, not of revelation or illumination. They are one continuous process, an unceasing battle, an indeterminate progress, an apprenticeship and a conquest—like freedom and love—which, taking place every day, is one of man over himself and that Nature to which he belongs.

My nystagmus lessened, becoming finally an almost imperceptible case of diverging strabismus. I gradually increased my reading exercises. Each day I read a bit more. Within a few weeks I was again entrusted to perform small tasks. In a month, two months—I don't know—I tackled fervently the story that I had conceived and to which during those nights in Bellevue Hospital I mentally gave shape (contrary to habit) down to the smallest detail. I wrote the story in two days. Its style—excited, euphoric—conveys, perhaps, my physical and mental state during that period. But the story was the fruit of impulses marked by ardent secular prayer and an immense hope that I might yet return and become a participant.

I walked, like a drunkard—with a rolling gait, dropping off to the left. If, while walking, I raised my eyes or turned my head, I lost my balance. To look up at a window or at the moon (which still danced in the sky, sometimes in tandem) I would have to stop and stare—resolutely, fixedly. Stars and distant lights seemed to me to be out of focus, my vision subaquatic, and lateral images were distinctly doubled. What I could take in a glance was diminished, and out in the streets any moving body quickly alarmed me. Bewilderment, buzzing in my ears and a touch of deafness, pains in my head, touchiness, patches of body insensibility when tired—all this remained with me. When I caught even the slightest of colds everything got worse. I submitted to several repetitive cures for my nose. Again I listened to specialists who—some of them—insisted that it would take an operation to correct my septum and one of the bony scales in the nose. Other doctors insisted that an operation would do me no good whatsoever. My bodily temperature shot up easily, putting me in a state of excitation and quasi-euphoria. I would alternate a few hours of work with many more hours of enforced rest. I disciplined myself to lie in bed—waiting patiently, silently, motionlessly, when my innermost being, with an intolerable desire for action, wanted only to launch itself into the world of the living.

Then, to overcome the fear of relapse, the dejection that comes with immobility, and the gloomy idea that I might turn into something of a cripple or invalid, I would close my eyes and repeat, "I have been much worse than this, and got better. This will pass. I must be calm." Sometimes it was difficult. But when the crisis was over (to this day I am like that) I felt an immense emotional gratitude to science and to life.

Amidst anxiety, suffering, and a diminished ability to deal with persons, I learned to control the useless excesses of revolt and to live within the feasible, the possible. I might not be up to "ninety percent of my old self," as the Master had predicted, but my actual seventy-five percent seemed to be more than sufficient for the now quite modest purposes to which I had scaled down my ambition. My imagination, the gifts of observation and evocation, my humor, and the capacity for expression were all intact, perhaps even honed.

I had detached myself some. I put that solitude to good advantage by once again turning into an insatiable reader, even more of one than before. But bit by bit I returned to an active, if still limited, life, to living among people.

For a year or more I had found myself compelled to walk with a rubber-tipped cane to correct my disequilibrium. The cane, an elegant accessory, has now fallen into disuse. It has become a sign of "rule and command" that irritates many good people. I would overhear remarks and gibes made by rude persons who, seeing me walk with agility and unable to guess at what my apparent physical vigor was hiding, supposed that I was a dandy and a parasite. There were those beings, too, who imagined that I hid behind my cane, exaggerating my need for it so that I might pass for an invalid. The most difficult thing in such situations is to make others comprehend that to live our lives we must now sometimes employ different techniques, reducing our motions somewhat, even though we continue to give them the illusion, as we move among them, that our energy and vitality are still intact. I got into the habit of smiling understandingly. It is incumbent upon us to choose between passing for "normal" and suffering the consequences of so doing—or revealing that we are damaged and then tolerating the pity and cruelty of others.

Intensely and joyfully I practiced at being and looking normal. I took endless walks. The first of them I took while still in New York in the company of Dr. Manuel de Azevedo Gomes, a young surgeon and orthopedist who was then serving brilliantly as an intern at the Orthopedics Hospital. With perfect tact and without my suspecting it, he put me deftly to the first test of my physical recuperation during a lengthy walk in Central Park.

For me life had the new taste of something relearned, something reconquered. I now wanted to live, not only for the pleasure of being alive, but to do all that which, until then, had been merely dream and promise. The terror of death, if I ever had it, had now transfigured itself into a fear that I would not live long enough or have the energy to make up for my dissipated past.

Close to ninety and only a step or two from the tomb, my mother had turned to me one day, as she sat before a window, and said, "Death does not frighten me. But I am sorry to leave all this, this blue sky, these trees—they are so green."

There were tears in her eyes. It is so beautiful—this stubborn persistence, this elementary, instinctive desire to remain alive, to be conscious—this resistance, this opposition to annihilation, despite fatigue, pain, and disappointment. Life has intrinsic merit, and if we can discern any purpose in life, it is this: perpetuate yourself, be fruitful, multiply.

I returned to Portugal for a time, traveled a bit more, reverted to living with some of my old illusions, errors, and beliefs, and underwent new crises. A few years later, I kept an anxious and distant watch on Foster Kennedy's long final illness. His death bereaved me. He was followed in death by Dr. Friedman, and later by the surgeon Dr. Isaacs, that son of poor Lower East Side Jews. It is strange how we are affected by the deaths of those to whom we owe the saving of our lives. It is like being orphaned.

But let me backtrack a little.

Months after I left the hospital, but while I was still in New York, I went to the cinema for the first time since my illness. Movies provided the toughest of tests for my eye muscles, which continually failed to make the thousand slight movements necessary for adjustment to any rapid succession of images. While returning home (it was late), I noticed that along my street—West Seventeenth—a heavy immobile cloud of smoke stood over the neighborhood. I was alarmed. At that season the buildings were no longer being heated. In any case, it is certain that no janitor would be feeding the furnace at that forsaken hour. "It could be a fire!" I said to my wife, and started to run, limping but supported by my cane, until I reached the house across the street. I saw then that the smoke was coming from the neighboring building, the five floors of which were unoccupied except for the first, which housed a radiologist's offices.

I stopped to look at the spectacle. At the top of the outside steps (the stoop) and through the beveled windows of the tall, double old-style doors, I spotted a tremendous blaze. The elaborate woodwork in the vestibule and on the first flight of stairs was burning away serenely, giving the street the majestic impression that it was an immense altar—illuminated, in flames—a painting of imprisoned fire.

There is nothing more thrilling than a fire in the night, burning in solitude, silence, darkness. In Lisbon I had witnessed several notable fires, and in Brussels I had seen the burning of the Grande Hôtel de la Bourse, an event that inspired an episode in one of my novellas. But though I had lived for eleven years in New York, where fires are frequent and spectacular and where at every moment firetrucks sounding their apocalyptic din race through the streets and the avenues, I had never before seen the burning of a building. (I hope that no one will now think that I have an incendiary's instincts.)

That old, near-vacant, five-story building was in the courts and must have been insured. Its burning did not endanger any human life. It was just a bonfire in the dark of night. I felt greatly tempted just to watch the whole building burn down. For a few moments I did watch—I could almost hear the flames crackle through the two doors with the thick glass—and I thought: given all that dry wood and with the staircase serving as a draft chimney, the fire will soon consume the building from top to bottom, reducing it to debris. Then suddenly it occurred to me that the flames might spread to the neighboring houses—to ours, to the very side where on the top floor our daughter, alone, was sleeping! I was frightened. I looked around me. Other than ourselves there wasn't a living thing on the street, not one soul or a single shop (everything was closed).

I ran to the corner of Second Avenue, found a standing taxi, banged on the window, and screamed at the driver: "There's a fire!"

The man was talking to a young girl sitting in the back seat. He gestured brusquely, and said, "Beat it!"

Then on the opposite corner I spotted a fire-alarm box, topped by its lit-up orange globe. (I had never noticed it before.) I crossed the avenue and for the first time in my life I felt the pride and pleasure—and believe me it is a pleasure—one has when pulling the lever. A furious alarm was set off, and in less than a minute and a half firetrucks filled the neighborhood with their customary fanfare of sirens and bells.

It occurred to me then to turn myself—in a childlike gesture—into a scout. I advanced to the center of the intersection and like an emergency flagman, raised my thick cane, pointing the firemen to the fire. With amazing docility and efficiency they obeyed me. How proudly did I play my ephemeral role as savior! (I was only forty-four. There's always time to begin anew.)

The taxi had disappeared. Seeing the street full of fire-fighting equipment—resplendent metal in white and brilliant reds, flashing, revolving beacons, and uncoiled hose—along with some curiosity-seekers, I made my way to an enormous, red-faced policeman. I informed him that it was I who had turned in the alarm—the act, in short, of a dutiful citizen. This giant looked at me indifferently, and without a word turned his back on me. It was as if he had said to me, "Listen, don't be a meddler. It might cost you—plenty." That policeman did me a great service. What a pickle I could have gotten into! Only much later did I understand that. No one said a word about the fire, which fifteen minutes later was out.

The whole thing intrigued me. The empty building was in litigation. Somewhere in all this, wasn't there the hand of an arsonist, a sinister firebug? The following day I went over to see the damage. The complicated woodwork of those elegant antique stairs—molding, adornments, flourishes, the banister—was charred all the way from the vestibule to the top floor. With my "detective's instinct" and the memory of long-past readings of a technical-legal nature, I looked at the stair landing and concluded that the fire had started in a chair, stuffed with parchment or some such thing. The chair, which was in a corner on the side opposite the entrance to the doctor's offices, was reduced nearly to rubbish. How, at that hour of the night in an empty house, could a fire have broken out in a chimney-bench?

I was then accosted by the radiologist's nurse. She was young, pretty, colored. "Are you looking for something?"

I told her that I was just looking over the damage, and then deliberately I added (was it done in vanity or out of innocence?): "I was the one who discovered the fire and called it in."

She looked surprised, and smiled, "Ah well, the doctor will want to thank you."

I entered the building and the radiologist came out to meet me among all that ancient and beat-up apparatus. He was tall, pale, puffy, and taciturn. He thanked me unenthusiastically and said, "I was working here with some people until after midnight. Somebody must have dropped a burning cigarette butt."

As I left I could not help thinking, "Who the devil does he bring in here at all hours of the night that is so careless? Was this done for the insurance?"

I am not inventing narrative for a novella. This incident, in which my cane played a decisive role (that's why I'm telling it), and the description of which caused me pleasurable difficulty, I took to calling "The night I set myself up as a boy scout and saved a burning building."

Upon returning to New York after spending nearly a year (1949–50) in Brazil, I one day decided to give up my cane once and for all. I broke it in two by striking it violently against a tree or a pole—I don't really know which. Later there were many times when I missed my cane and regretted having done what I did, but I was determined to renounce all props, to stop compromising with my weakness, to stop arousing hostility and commiseration, and to stop turning myself into a spectacle for the eyes of my fellow creature, my "other," and—at times—my wolf.

Even after so many years, especially when I am tired—if I cross a street in threatening traffic, if I am walking in the dark or over rough terrain where I lose my balance and stumble—I still resort mentally to a crook or staff to hold myself up. But I overcome this temptation and silently put up with my deficiency as well as I can. There are so many beautiful things around us, and so much to do!

Apropos of this, I recall that years ago, as I was about to enter a bus on Third Avenue, the one that goes to the Bowery and is much used by the sad people of that part of the city, I tried to help a cripple on crutches, just ahead of me, get on the bus. The man scurrilously spurned my help and vexedly made me board the bus ahead of him. I was perplexed. When I got home I commented on the matter. My daughter had been with me, and with the perspicacity proper to those of the James Dean generation and in the severity with which children today correct their antiquated parents, said to me, "The man was right, Dad. You made him feel like a cripple."

That lesson stayed with me. One does well to learn from young people, those who have that observational freshness we perhaps no longer have. What we so often take for expressions of goodness and charity are merely cruel reminders to those who, straining to forget that they are maimed, are trying to adjust themselves to their relative "inferiority" so that they will not be considered "beings apart." All that we accomplish is to revivify their consciousness of their condition. We humiliate them so that we can flatter our own pride as humanitarians. Our notion of what is "humane" has some unexpected facets.

Instead of looking to remind our fellow creatures of their defects, their sore spots, and their "inferiority"—they who have the right to live as best they know how (and this applies in particular to a culture vitiated to the marrow by a spirit of censure and depreciation, by intolerance, backbiting, and the vice of insisting on "ideal perfection")—would we not be doing better (and behaving more humanely) if we tried to put into relief, stimulate, and cultivate that which in each individual is salvageable, healthy, creative, and original? To arouse in that individual the desire to persist in those very things? Who can consider himself so free of defects that he can set up as the intransigent judge of his fellow creatures? We have much to learn.

But it's time to finish.

I had entered Bellevue Hospital, prostrate with pain, my morale smashed, with one foot in the grave, and I had readied myself for death, crossing internally that fateful barrier that separates the living from the dead. I had confronted and accepted my probable destiny—with half a face and half a smile. I had cut loose, in short, from the moorings of life—desires, plans, intentions—so that I could integrate myself into that small universe that is the infirmary, that species of train with sealed orders that drops off its passengers, one after the other, at the stops on the Sans-End line. And I can claim without vanity or shame that it was easy, simple, and natural. In that action there was no anxiety, no fear.

This, perhaps, is the greatest lesson. Death had lost its magical, frightening power. Organically, we belong to the animal and plant world. Have you ever seen an old cat die—hunched in a corner, withdrawn into itself, like someone fulfilling a serious mission? We are exactly like that. I have witnessed the deaths of persons who had agonized painfully for months, and in every case the process was the same.

Concentrating on his combat, obsessed by it, the patient seems to break with the world to accept the temporary, decisive, and solitary mission of battling for survival. And suddenly, when his strength fails and his illness gets the better of him, even this he gives up. It is as if his consciousness has accepted dissolution, and he has given himself up to the current, descending serenely without shock and bump into the drift of the great tame river that rolls, ever more darkly, ever wider and deeper, until it merges with the immeasurable ocean that is our source and to which, having fulfilled the cycle of personal existence, we irresistibly, inexorably return. And this, you can believe, is not hard at all.

In death, as in life, what hurts us above all and humiliates us most is useless rebellion. Acceptance of the ineluctable, however, is pacifying.

If, however, we are obsessedly anxious to endure, we should be appeased by the idea that each one of us has brought with him, at birth, a promise and a portion of perpetuity. Each one of us is a link in the biological chain that continues the species, stretching back to the watery basis of time—the amoebas and the algae—and remaining obstinately on the road to the future. Life, like an inextinguishable spark, jumps from vessel to vessel, from being to being, such that the prodigious chain will not be interrupted.

Life is not a personal privilege. It is something that goes beyond us as individuals. It belongs to nature, to history, to society. It is of men as a "whole," in space and time, that true eternity is made. And it is only among them, in society, consciousness, and action, that we feel real and are real.

That is why, at a distance of years and after all I have experienced—despite my momentary revolt and resignation to the ineluctable—I say that it is much better to have returned to life, to have come back to hope and belief, and to accomplish things to the measure of one's personal potential.

Under hope's spell, pain itself turns into a myth.

Lisbon, November 1957.

Library of Congress Cataloging-in-Publication Data

Miguéis, José Rodrigues, 1901–
    [Homem sorri à morte, com meia cara. English]
    A man smiles at death with half a face / José Rodrigues Miguéis;
translated and with an introduction by George Monteiro.
    p. cm.
    Translation of: Um homem sorri à morte, com meia cara.
    Includes bibliographical references.
    ISBN 0-87451-503-3
    1. Physician and patient—Fiction. 2. Terminally ill—Fiction.
I. Title.
PQ9261.M568H6613   1990
869.3′41—dc20

                                       90-38976
                                           CIP